DANCING

WITH YOUR

MUSE

Gilda Joffe, graduate of The Juilliard School, is an executive coach for women, with a specialty in eliminating fears hindering development of business and creative potential. With a focus on mindset work, she has over 25 years of teaching and coaching experience and is a certified HeartMath® trainer for businesses and individuals.

As a violinist, Gilda performed throughout North America, as well as internationally with various European ensembles in major halls across the world.

You can find out more about Gilda at performermindset.com.

GILDA JOFFE

DANCING
WITH YOUR
MUSE

Inner magic to release fear
and embrace creativity

First published 2021

Exisle Publishing Pty Ltd
PO Box 864, Chatswood, NSW 2057, Australia
226 High Street, Dunedin, 9016, New Zealand
www.exislepublishing.com

A CiP record for this book is available from the National Library of Australia.

ISBN 978-1-922539-06-9

Designed by Enni Tuomisalo
Typeset in PT Serif, 10 pt
Printed in China

This book uses paper sourced under ISO 14001 guidelines from well-managed forests and other controlled sources.

10 9 8 7 6 5 4 3 2 1

Disclaimer
While this book is intended as a general information resource and all care has been taken in compiling the contents, neither the author nor the publisher and their distributors can be held responsible for any loss, claim or action that may arise from reliance on the information contained in this book. As each person and situation is unique, it is the responsibility of the reader to consult a qualified professional regarding their personal care.

To my beloved husband,
the most constantly curious
and creative person I know!

Contents

PART 3: SUCCESS IN DIFFERENT GUISES

PART 4: WRAPPING IT UP FOR COSMIC SEND-OFF

Preface

When my grandmother was born, many fairies came to her cradle and delivered practically an embarrassment of gifts. She was given prodigious musical talent, an affinity for dance, a head for mathematics and an eye for drawing, as well as a large dose of charm, wit and beauty. When the last fairy came to visit her, she made the daunting pronouncement that my grandmother would never be able to fulfill the potential of any of these talents. Unfortunately, life events as well as personal decisions did subsequently prove this to be true.

Whenever we *really* want to pursue something, all of us have the ability to find strong reasons why it might not work or succeed. We have an exquisite capacity to back up those misconceptions with superb rationalizations and irrational emotional states, thus perfectly preventing us from reaching what we most desire.

Guilt, fear and self-deception are some of the many ways people suppress within themselves that which so richly deserves expression. But each of us, no matter our life path, has something of creative value and importance which needs to be brought forth, not only as an ardent expression of our own psyche, but as a shimmering light for others.

It may seem impossible at times to fight against the voices of our own personal histories and self-doubts or the noisy judgments of others when attempting to express ourselves in a creative manner. And yet not to try is to experience, somewhere along the line, inner pain and sadness.

I have heard so many times 'I really wanted to but ...', 'It was always my dream, however I was told ...' 'Oh I couldn't possibly do that ...' or 'I'm just not very creative ...'. These are revealing statements in themselves.

There are many reasons why people give up their dreams. Not just the big ones, but also the colorful, smaller visions which, like facets of a jewel, would sparkle if brought to light.

The terror of being forced to perform in the yearly recital at the home of my music teacher brought equal parts crippling fear and nasty physical symptoms, plus a strange sensation of feeling myself to be two people at the same time, in the same body: the twelve-year-old I was and, in some dimly recognizable form, my future adult self. I realized in later years that the origin of this peculiar feeling was my higher awareness, which seemed to have momentarily popped in to reassure a very nervous kid. This consciousness, while responsive to my discomfort, probably knew it would have to wait a long time for my younger self to discover her own powers. Especially that particular power, belonging to all of us, which transforms anxiety into confident self-expression.

But that day, at the beginning of the morning, I felt only pangs of anxiety which even the most optimistic bird tweets outside my window did not alleviate.

Arriving later in the day at my teacher's home, with its nineteenth-century high-ceilinged living room, creaky floors and dim rickety floor lamps hugging the piano, it was evident that I had the scary distinction of being the youngest among the 'older' students of sixteen and seventeen. Closer to the moment of performance, my heart pounded most uncomfortably and my hands became even more stiff, cold and sweaty from clutching my instrument. Worst of all, the voice of my music teacher started to bellow in my direction.

Being an expert at worrying way ahead of time, I was terrified of not playing well. A scenario of humiliation, disgrace and possible expulsion was definitely possible, since I had witnessed that exact circumstance happen to other students in the past. My music dreams would be over, I would have to quit, the future was doomed ...!

Fortuitously, the bellowing veered off from my part of the room and landed instead on another miserable-looking candidate. Relief came, but not much, knowing that although I had gained some moments of safety, the trial was still ahead. As this other unhappy student took up his instrument, I scanned his face, noticing my own terror well reflected in his expression. Surprisingly however, as he began to play, a slow feeling of calm, which was completely unexpected, began to creep over me. My nervousness started to evaporate. Perhaps it was because he carried so much anxiety that it was not necessary for me to carry as much myself. He had enough for both! But *because* of the calmness that began to come over me, I had a curious realization, and it was that indelible moment which became the basis of this book.

During many youthful recitals I struggled with various conflicts having nothing to do with the music, but everything to do with the issues that I see in my teenage and adult clients today. Wanting to be seen, afraid to be seen, self-esteem, fear of judgment, peer pressure, negative head voices, fear of success, fear of failure. The list drones on.

These are conflicts that everyone experiences who is trapped by fear and the countless 'reasons' why we cannot have our longed-for desires. Many of those reasons can be eliminated by the understanding and acceptance that there absolutely exist alternate routes to our wishes. This occurs especially if we choose to say yes even to strange-looking opportunities, which might not be easy to spot or even look like opportunities at times. However, accepting them can lead us to places we might never have imagined could be as intriguing, or desirous, as the destinations themselves.

There isn't a person alive who hasn't experienced the effects of fear at some moment when it comes to personal choices or expectations from others. However, fear is just an emotion translated into bodily feelings. It is created by us, and it can be transformed by us into the needed fuel to start or propel our hopes into amazing living realities. Even in the middle of chaos we can nourish the small dream spark and keep it alive until the time when it can burst into transformative flames. In fact, chaos itself can sometimes be a most magnificent (albeit painful) catalyst in bringing forth previously hidden, but helpful, insights.

The recital realization, and what I continued to learn over the following years, led to wonderful and gratifying professional and personal outcomes. Ten years after that anguished event, I did indeed become a professional musician, playing concerts everywhere, living and traveling in many countries and, later — most rewarding of all — working with hundreds of students and clients from all professions and stages of life, in the areas of peak performance and development of creative potential. Helping people to travel the tremendous peaks and valleys that come with any dream, and to more easily surf their own waves of experience, has been my greatest joy.

Understanding our fears and how they hold us back is the first step in waving the magic wand over our delusions of smallness, so that we may recognizably transform ourselves back into the powerful beings that we already are.

In these pages we will discover how to step off the false emotional roads which take us away from our most wished-for destinations. Instead, we will learn to courageously choose the most direct pathways to creative success and, more importantly, personal fulfillment, no matter what our background, profession or present situation.

So, what *was* the sudden awareness discovered so long ago at that agonizing recital?

It was in realizing that if a person could be so miserable in a single moment and completely calm in the next, it meant only one thing ... that I was in control. The condition of my mind and thoughts was completely up to me. *That mind defines destiny.*

It was a huge, fortunate perception for a twelve year old, and a gift with which I have worked ever since.

How we think determines our behaviors and actions. Nothing else.

Thought precedes all. Knowing that we have control over what we think seems trite and obvious. However, most people go through their entire lives without realizing the profound implications of this knowledge.

How often we blame others for how we feel, never understanding that our emotions are created solely by ourselves. Of course, we must never stay or participate in circumstances that threaten our physical or emotional welfare. However, in normal day-to-day life our behaviors are dictated solely by our emotions, which arrive directly from our thoughts.

Therefore, it is of paramount importance that what we think is of the most emotionally nutritious nature if we are to have happy and creative lives. Our whole existence is one of creativity from the moment we get up in the morning until we rest our bodies and minds at night.

All of us yearn in some way to express ourselves through our interests, whether that be through the potter's wheel, a painting class, designing gardens, writing, playing music, learning a dance, cooking a delicious meal or a million other possibilities that we who are so fortunate to be alive can choose! The only thing that can prevent us from enjoying this soul expression is ourselves. And the one emotion that can cause us so much distress in all areas of our lives is fear.

Fear has many forms besides those with which we are familiar. It can slip in uninvited under other emotions, such as anger or envy. Sometimes we may not even know that we are afraid of something, unless we dig a little within ourselves to explore what lies at the bottom of our reactions.

Most of us are nervous about stepping beyond what is 'acceptable' in terms of 'expressing ourselves'. Add to this the fact that our various cultures and upbringings all have different 'rules' and we begin to feel constrained before we even begin!

Ironically, those in professions who receive the most public adoration are generally mavericks who have let their creativity burst forth in a way which the rest of us generally do not allow ourselves to do. Like them or not, our present-day entertainers, big personality sports figures and tech inventors of the latest and greatest capture our imaginations precisely because we let ourselves live emotionally through their personalities and accomplishments.

However, we don't have to *be* them, nor do we need society's permission to access our own sources of creativity.

No matter our background or profession, the desire or need to express oneself creatively should be of great importance in our own eyes. And we must realize that our decision to do so is far more important than *any* worldly judgments, negative or positive, which may occur or be expressed as a result of our actions and creations.

What this means is that *we* are the only ones who have the right to give permission to our expressive yearnings, whether that means a presentation to a board, a performance on stage, a painting, project, poem or (most difficult and gratifying) learning to communicate wholeheartedly with another human being. It is not for outside voices to give us permission to plumb our own depths. We are the ones who hold the keys to our own creative kingdoms.

Dancing with Your Muse is a series of essays, divided into four parts. Part 1, 'Fear in all its glory', speaks to many of the most prevalent inner fears which assail us the instant we even think of moving forwards towards our creative hopes and dreams. By understanding these common fears we realize we are not alone and that we are indeed capable of transforming these inhibitors into positive outcomes. In Part 2, 'Judgment and criticism', we discuss the pressures and anxieties felt as a result of external influences, and how to keep ourselves in balance without succumbing to outside perceptions of our worth. Part 3, 'Success in different guises', expands our notions of success by more personal understanding of what accomplishment means to us, and how this knowledge can deliver confidence, self-compassion and previously unseen possibilities. In the final section, 'Wrapping it up for cosmic send-off', we look at the larger picture, realizing the gifts of our own being, and how lucky each of us is to be a color in the great portrait of humanity. Personal stories, with names changed to protect privacy, are sprinkled throughout the book to help highlight specific fears and/or solutions.

We will learn that creativity is a process, not a 'thing', and that we are all endowed with this miraculous gift. Learning how to dance with creation and its myriad possibilities is what helps us to sail through the turbulent seas on our life voyages.

Having come into life we may therefore express what has been given to us … to feel the value and divinity of that which we individually possess. To be here for the instinctual joy of delivering to the world, in humbleness and thanks, that which has been gifted to us in our dreams, our visions, and in our hearts by the great unknown which created us.

Introduction:
We made it!

Congratulations! Just by being delivered here to planet Earth, means that we are packages of incredible possibilities waiting to be opened ... by us!

Somewhere or other, the idea might have gotten drummed into our heads that we had to be Michelangelo or Leonardo da Vinci in order to allow ourselves to do anything imaginative or expressive. We think perhaps that whatever we do must be accepted and validated by others, or by people who are 'in the know', in order to be considered valuable.

Very early on in first grade Mallory was making a Valentine's card for her mother along with the rest of the children in her class. She spent time happily cutting out her little red hearts, pasted with bits of paper lace and decorated with big, colorful, magic marker flowers. All of Mallory's little being was excited and looking forward to how much her mother would enjoy receiving the card.

When everyone was finished and the teacher came around to

look at the cards, she looked at Mallory's with a surprised expression on her face and exclaimed, 'You are not going to give *that* to your mother, are you?' Mallory was absolutely crushed ... and without a word took her card and trotted over to the rubbish bin where she promptly dropped it in. Since that long ago day, Mallory has felt she could never do anything worthwhile in art and therefore stopped giving herself permission to try.

So many of us have experienced inner or outer voices which do, or don't, give us permission to ignite our own passions. Events in life can close down our portals to expression and create doubts about our 'right' to be creative, especially when we compare ourselves to others.

Typically, people will say 'Oh, I'm just not creative, I don't have any talent, so it's not fun' (as if having talent has anything to do with having fun), 'I can't carry a tune', 'the only artistic brush I use is to sweep cat hair off the sofa', 'so and so is the talented one in the family', 'I'm too old', etc.

" "

*Creativity is inventing, experimenting,
growing, taking risks, breaking rules,
making mistakes, and having fun.*

Mary Lou Cook

But creativity is our birthright.

If you have ever watched a very young toddler trying to get out of their cot you will have noticed that he or she is extraordinarily inventive in the ways they manage to wriggle up to, and straddle, the corners of the bed in an attempt to get their leg over the bars to escape — many times with success, much to the chagrin of their parents! But nobody has said to them, 'You don't have the brains or imagination to figure a way out of this, so just stay put!'

To understand a little of your connection with (and fear of) imaginatively expressing yourself as well as discovering what has helped or hindered you, you might think over the following questions, since how we relate to our creativity illustrates how we relate to ourselves and our lives.

TO PONDER

> What do I feel about my relationship with creativity?

> How did I come to this conclusion? (what events in my life caused me to think this way?)

> How do I look at myself objectively as a creative person?

> Did I have a time, moment, period in my life where I really wished to express myself in a certain creative way, but did not dare?

> What were some of the reasons why I couldn't fulfill that wish/goal?

> What was the emotional cost to me in my life of not fulfilling that desire, even in a small way?

There are as many ways to answer these questions as there are blades of grass, but typically people begin with their feelings. 'I felt like the untalented middle child', 'I felt I wasn't the creative one, since my partner was the successful artist', 'I was the youngest and I felt guilty for even wanting art lessons when there was no money', 'I was too shy and was afraid to ask for what I wanted/needed' or 'I was terrified of being judged and criticized'.

TO PONDER

> If you were able to chant a spell, instantly allowing you to have the life of your creative dreams or simply to have more creative outlets, large or small in your daily life:

> What would your outcomes look like?

> Would you be inspired by solitude or by connecting and collaborating with others?

> What perceived obstacles or barriers would your magic wand defeat?

> How have previous attempts to express your hopes and desires frustrated you? Or inspired you?

It is not necessary that you find concrete answers to all the questions above. They are only meant as catalysts to stir your emotions and to allow thoughts to come bubbling up which otherwise may not have surfaced. Like the old fairy tale of Rumpelstiltskin, when we know the name of something it no longer has power over us. When we are able to access our emotions, showing us how we really feel towards our creative selves, we can learn to give less importance to outer events, and be encouraged to turn inwards, developing our deeper powers of vision and expressivity.

""

Everything you can imagine is real.

Pablo Picasso

TIME TO RIP OFF THE WRAPPING PAPER!

Strategic decisions, visual art displays, writing, performing arts, scientific research, flower arrangements, the sports arena, public speaking, and even deciding how to arrange the laundry piles or when to feed the dog are among the hundreds of daily large and small creative acts that we participate in every day. In fact, every decision of our day and our lives involves some creative thought. We cannot help but create.

Let us see how working through some very common feelings and attitudes can propel us into a future of realized goals, fun and fulfillment!

PART 1: FEAR IN ALL ITS GLORY

1.

What the heck is fear?

"

You can't stop the waves,
but you can learn to surf.

Jon Kabat-Zinn

Peter is standing outside the imposing soundproof stage door, waiting to cross its threshold onto a large stage where he will perform a high-stakes orchestral audition. After a five-hour flight the previous day, he has been practicing practically all night in his hotel room using an instrument mute that makes him sound like a mosquito, since it's the only device that will allow him to play without having all the other hotel guests banging on his door.

He knows that this is his *only* chance to win this position. He has been practicing and sweating about this audition for months, preparing five to six hours a day, performing mock auditions in front of others, worrying, overthinking and finally the moment is here!

Standing outside that door before he goes in, he feels beyond nervous. He knows what is at stake. It doesn't matter about all his previous preparation. All he can think about is how nervous he feels. And how afraid he is of the fear itself! In fact, being afraid of the fear and how it will affect his playing is just as alarming as the audition. So he has double fear to worry about. He adjusts his instrument, making sure all his cello strings are in tune; his pianist is ready, the large doors swing open, letting out the smiling and confident face of the other competitor, and just as he is about to step through the door onto the huge stage … one of his cello strings snaps!

Fear generally serves to protect us in situations which may affect our survival. In ancient times, our fear protected us from hungry wild animals by sending cascades of chemicals into our systems that allowed us to fight or flee (triggering what's known as the fight or flight response). Today, those chemical deluges are also vitally necessary when we dart back from a car rushing towards us as we cross the street.

However, sometimes fear can be an inappropriate traveling companion. Those same chemical cascades that helped us to avoid danger are much more destructive and wearing to our bodies in non-life-threatening situations such as stage performances, public speaking or year-end reviews, where we find it is not easy to turn off the reactions of rapid heartbeat, sweaty palms and shaky hands, even though we know in our heads that we will survive.

But why *do* we feel fear? According to scientific research it happens, simply enough, when an anxiety-provoking event occurs in our external environment. This produces a signal, which is immediately sent to the oldest, most primitive part of our brain. If it is scared enough, it will send messages to the body that 'this is serious' and to prepare for fight or flight mode. As a result, higher decision-making capabilities are shut down and the primary focus becomes survival. That is why, under stressful circumstances people will often say, when asked about something not pertaining to the situation at hand, 'I … I can't think about that right now …!'

And they are absolutely right. They cannot think about other subjects until the 'danger' has passed and they have regained total brain capability.

Although Peter knew intellectually that this was not about survival, his hormonal system reacted otherwise, and since he could not (or chose not to!) flee or run from the 'danger', he ended up with surges of chemicals flowing throughout his body. He said that he had so much adrenaline just before playing that he probably could have run several miles around the building without even panting. Unfortunately, there was no place for all those fight or flight chemicals to escape, except into various body parts, thus inhibiting his natural relaxed movements and making him stiff as a board.

There were many ways *my* musical colleagues handled similar fears and stress, most of which were not helpful in the long run. I once saw a prominent oboist, whose hands were shaking pre-concert, proceed to down an entire bottle of wine as if it were grape juice, minutes before he went on stage. He did manage to play his entrances correctly, but his liver expired much earlier than his orchestral contract.

Most of our fears are like barnacles: acquired through life experiences. Therefore it is interesting to learn that babies come into this world with only two inborn fears: the fear of falling and the fear of loud noises. As we mature we become experts at creating internal scenarios of doom which usually never occur.

" "

I am an old man and have known a great many troubles, but most of them never happened.

Mark Twain

A CONVERSATION WITH THE HEART

There are ways of handling the anxiety towards a fearful situation that you know in advance is coming your way. One of the best ways to do this is to have a conversation with the part of yourself that has the deepest knowing … the heart.

According to Rollin McCraty, PhD, director of research at the HeartMath® Institute in Boulder Creek, California, 'the heart actually sends more information to the brain, neurologically speaking, than the brain to the heart'. The heart is the seat of our emotions, because of its connection with our autonomic nervous system. And because of that, it contains a vast amount of knowledge which is not accessed through intellect but through feelings.

In contemplating a particular future situation, you might want to ask yourself the following questions — not all at once, but giving time for the answers to emerge, so that they may come on their own, unrushed and richer in intuitive information.

TO PONDER

> Will a negative outcome of this situation truly affect my life in a permanent manner? Or is it just one of many possibilities on the road to my goals?

> Is my caring about it true balanced care, or am I magnifying it so much that it becomes 'over-care' and therefore harmful to my mind and body?

> Am I creating irrational scenarios in my mind based on the past, which have nothing to do with the future?

> Do I trust in myself and the infinite possibilities which are always ahead?

Most people going into a stressful situation imagine one specific result that they must have as the key to getting what they want. However, when you stop basing your ideas of success on one specific result you start to encounter success through other previously unseen possibilities.

When Peter's string broke, he felt that everything was over ... that there was no point trying to think positively since having to change a string on his cello at such an important moment meant constant readjustment would be necessary to play in tune. And that was certainly not what he needed in a crucial seven-minute audition. He returned to the side room to change his string, and for the moment another contestant took his place. He didn't have time to ask himself profound questions. But in the minutes he did have, he found himself reassessing his attitudes about the whole situation.

When he returned to his place outside the audition door, he felt much calmer and really not very nervous at all.

So what happened? He had made a calculated inner change ...

Plain and simple, he gave up his investment in fear. An awfulness had already happened. There was nothing to do but go on. He wasn't giving up ... he was giving *in* to whatever might happen and became accepting of whatever might occur, trusting in himself and his future.

And the outcome? It turned out to be one of the best auditions of his life. He won the position and stayed in that orchestra for a great many years.

Everyone wants to get rid of one thing and gain something else. But two emotions, such as fear and courage, cannot be held at the same time. In order to have courage you need to release fear, since the universe will not give you something unless you make a place for it.

The reason I felt compelled to write this book was to make sure that (unlike Peter and many others) you don't have to wait for inspiration to come and hit you over the head in the middle of stress. By working with the above questions, you can prepare yourself long before an expected challenging situation. In doing so, you will discover answers that will create more realistic scenarios, thereby supporting you emotionally and enabling you to present your best self.

2.

First steps versus no steps

""

If not now, when?

The Talmud

Watching a young child learn to walk is a heart-filling and joyous sight! Why do we consistently feel that emotion? Perhaps because we see the potential and exciting future that lie in wait for them after they achieve the success we know will happen. They try, stagger, fall, begin again, always encouraged by the open arms of those who love them.

Self-judgment doesn't occur. There are no thoughts of 'Can I do this? Should I do this? Maybe I should try next year instead?' There is only a destination, whether a few feet or across the room, and a curious, joyous determination to get there.

As we mature, the list of pros and cons about doing something that we might wish to do becomes so heavy and confusing that sometimes we just give up on our ideas. The fear that we might 'fail' or 'not do it right' (whatever that means) or the notions of 'I don't have any talent for ...', 'I'm too ...' are such dampening thoughts it is amazing we actually get up in the morning to do anything!

Part of the definition of 'create' in the Merriam-Webster Dictionary is 'to make or produce (something): to cause (something new) to exist'. Something new ... something that did not exist before ... We cannot know in advance the outcomes of all the steps we take on our creative paths, for if we did, it would indeed cease to be *creative*! By taking small actions and relishing the joys, as well as the satisfactions in finding solutions to difficulties that inevitably arise, we begin to notice of what stuff we are made, and who we really are.

""

I'm a much better dancer in the studio than on stage. Why? Because I have more fun in the studio; it's the freedom, the learning, doing the last stages of a work. I'm much better dancing for a choreographer than for an audience.

Mikhail Baryshnikov

Finding ways to be creative is one way to discover the unknown facets of your being. Not being afraid to have atrocious results is the quickest way to find out more about yourself. The inevitable bumps and difficulties along the way are to be embraced, since they serve to sculpt us into the best versions of ourselves. No matter what it is that we wish to do — take a painting class, change professions, try a writing seminar, study a language, build sand castles, ask for a raise — we first need to give ourselves psychological permission. And that is exactly the point at which most people become stuck.

> *Finding ways to be creative is one way to discover the unknown facets of your being.*

TO PONDER

> Why is it so hard to give ourselves permission to do something our heart yearns for us to try?

> What itchy little fears are preventing us from taking that first small step towards our vision?

Perhaps there are voices from the past telling us we aren't talented enough to even think about our desires, or we tell ourselves, 'It's too late', 'It's not okay to focus on what I need' or one of my all-time favorite future-crushing excuses, 'because I don't know if I will succeed'!

But when we don't give ourselves permission to express ourselves, whether in a group meeting, private conversation, starting a new business venture or doing a sand sculpture, we are shutting down our life force. We could pay a great price if we close ourselves off from our most profound source of energy and inspiration — our spiritual selves.

We cannot shut down aspects of our inner being and expect that other emotional systems will function perfectly without them. Yes, we will bumble along day to day, but it will be without the expertise, wisdom and joy of those parts we have suppressed. We can go through an entire life without knowing who we really are, and that is indeed a sobering thought. But it need not be that way, since enjoying life and discovering oneself is an inside job!

Therefore, for emotional satisfaction (and good brain health!) it is important to move out of our usual experiences in order to discover different aspects of ourselves. In doing so, we discover completely new perspectives on how we might live our lives.

DISCOVERING WHO YOU ARE

Johan tried to do as much traveling as possible when living in London for two years while working for a large international corporation, since it was easy to visit neighboring countries owing to their proximity. He found that each culture he visited brought out different aspects of his personality, which made him wonder at times who he was! Flamenco dancing with abandonment in a café was not his 'normal' personality, but it happened (after much wine), much to his own amusement. No doubt he was probably beyond awful, he surmised; but in any case, he was definitely having a good time and was not too concerned with what other people might think. No one there knew him anyway, and since he was in Spain at the time, he could be 'another' person.

However, you don't have to travel to Spain to find out who you are. Sometimes, taking a small risk, in the sense of doing something completely out of your comfort range, can be the first turn of the key in the lock. You might try driving home using a completely different route, or deliberately set out to get lost, knowing of course that you will find your way back, perhaps a little later than usual!

Even a small escapade can get your mind and creative juices flowing. In fact, every time you learn something new or experience something different, new connections are made in the brain — which means that you *literally* become a different person!

The sooner you allow yourself to step off your usual paths even for an hour or two — perhaps to daydream or engage in something you have forever wanted to do but have never allowed yourself to think about as a possibility (developing some software, a glass-blowing class, designing a building, a fantastically 'ridiculous' new idea for your business, acting lessons, emotionally supporting someone who is stuck in a rut) — the more you become used to the idea of trying different things. This then becomes a positive new habit, helping to dispel previous negative feelings and self-pronouncements which might still be trying to hitch a ride.

"

*You don't have to see the whole
staircase, just take the first step.*

Martin Luther King

Each new choice we make leads us into the flow of creation, and eventually to our best destination. The most important step is to accept the invitation to the dance.

3.

Everyone says 'don't be nervous'

"

You wouldn't worry so much about
what others think of you if you
realized how seldom they do!

Olin Miller

How many times have you heard that completely useless phrase 'don't be nervous' uttered by well-meaning people? As if anyone wants to be nervous, or as if we absolutely *decide* to be nervous!

Therefore, on top of *feeling* nervous, we have to contend with other people's expectations that we should *not* be nervous! This added layer to the nervous cake means we now have the additional fear of how people will perceive us should we have the effrontery to actually be afraid. Phew, a lot to worry about.

What it boils down to is that on a very primitive level we are afraid that we will be outcasts because of our 'flaws'. Once we understand this, we can take a step back and not become so down on ourselves for what we are feeling. And we can realize that most of our daily stress situations, stage performances, decision-making, corporate presentations, public speaking, creative dilemmas, end-of-year reviews are *not* mortally dangerous ... except to our ego.

In general, though, when you hear someone say, 'There is no reason to be nervous' it is about as helpful as someone telling you that tarantulas make great pets when you have a tarantula phobia.

A few years ago, on a trip to the former Soviet Republic of Georgia, I was traveling with my husband and friends to a rather remote countryside ruin. Standing there among the old walls, with the wind blowing and singing among the stones, I suddenly heard a sound which raised my hackles. I had never really known where hackles were, but I distinctly felt them rise at that moment. I heard a sort of hissing from a direction I could not identify, a sound which I was not able to pair with any recognizable pattern in my brain. It disturbed me greatly.

I asked my dear husband if he had heard it and he answered that it was probably just cicadas. Now, I know cicadas from my childhood, and they never raised my mystery hackles. I looked all around, and found nothing ... but in slowly glancing around, and up, I saw a large serpent about two fingers width with its mouth open, hanging from an old vine trellis directly above my head.

I sprinted sideways with an Olympic ability I had never had before, and announced in a shrill, trembling voice that it was absolutely not cicadas! To my chagrin, everybody else found the snake 'fascinating', which is perhaps understandable when you realize they were quite a safe distance away.

You can be sure that anybody saying to me, 'Oh, don't be nervous, it's just a snake' would not have made the slightest difference in allaying the waves of adrenaline which coursed through my body, allowing me to make a 'graceful' sprint to the side.

But everyone copes with fear in different ways.

As another dancer, Rudolf Nureyev, said, 'Putting on my make-up, for example, is a way of becoming acquainted with the inevitable fact that I will have to go out and dance. I feel like cattle before slaughter. There is no escape. Really, what it boils down to is that we are paid for our fear.'[1]

DEALING WITH NERVES

Before standing on the podium for speaking events, Kathy used to calm herself by imagining herself doing household tasks, such as laundry and shopping, since it brought her down emotionally and psychologically to a mundane level of activity. In later years, she learned other more long-lasting methods of combatting public speaking nerves so that she would not have to resort to her grocery list!

Being nervous is not in itself a failure. In fact, I believe that one needs to have a slight 'edge' of exhilarating nervousness in order to do one's best. However, that kind of edge comes with clarity and slight excitement, not inability to function.

The best way to combat nervousness in any situation in which you need to 'present' yourself is to realize that the results, whatever they are, do *not* determine the rest of your life. It usually takes a bit of time for people to realize this, but after seeing the patterns in their own lives they eventually catch on to the fact that it is their own initiatives and decisions which turn out to be the huge turning points in their lives, and not the results of external events.

In other words, we have a great deal more control in how our lives turn out than we realize. It's always nice to learn this sooner than later (!) and, happily, I have had the opportunity to pass this nugget of wisdom on to others.

> *We have a great deal more control in how our lives turn out than we realize.*

In the positive sense, being nervous simply means that you care. We can, however, care in a way that takes into account the fact that no one event ever determines our fate. To do the best we can manage under any given circumstance is all that we need ever do. And if it isn't our very best at that moment, that's okay too!

Living is not about being at the top of our game all the time. It's about being in resonance with our potential, believing in it, nurturing it and being inspired by its possibilities. By feeling that power within ourselves, we take the long view and realize that opportunities for success are only limited by our beliefs. Therefore, by correctly cultivating our belief systems we harvest the future we desire.

TO PONDER

> Where have my beliefs about myself been created? At what time in my life? Under what circumstances?

> Would I be comfortable releasing old beliefs that proved to be untrue, knowing that this would affect my emotional state in a very positive way?

" "

The greatest weapon against stress is our ability to choose one thought over another.

William James

4.
Now you see me, now you don't

How often we hide ourselves. Behind careers, behind societal and family roles. Behind the titles we assume, Husband/Wife, Brother/Sister, Child/Parent, Boss/Employee, Friend/Acquaintance.

Do we really know ourselves? Do others know us? Or do we

show to others and ourselves only the parts that seem appropriate for the moment at hand?

Not easy questions. Probably not comfortable answers. However, certainly vital if we are to know who we are, and how we may contribute our very existence to the tapestry of humankind.

Most people naturally have different facets of themselves, which is why two friends of the same person may sometimes absolutely dislike each other, and cannot for the life of them understand what the mutual friend sees in the other.

However, sometimes people do not wish to be understood or seen by others, because they very often have an unconscious feeling that if they are really 'seen for who they are' they will:

> not be accepted
> be taken advantage of in some way
> be the unwanted center of attention
> be judged in some way which will undermine their self-esteem.

And the fact is that these fears might be absolutely reasonable.

We are tribal beings, in the sense that to be considered an outsider — or worse, not to be accepted by society — is one of the biggest fears we may have. You can see it on the playground among groups of children. Who is in? Who is out? It's the same in office politics, in societal cliques of all kinds.

People might try to take advantage of you in some way, until you learn to set appropriate boundaries.

You may or may not become the center of attention for positive or negative reasons; however, you still retain the choice of how you will react to that attention, and whether or not you choose to make it a part of your interior life.

You could be judged harshly by others who have no conception or understanding of who you are. But again, other people's conceptions of you have nothing to do with who you, in fact, are.

> *We are all much larger than our fears and possess more might and strength than our inherent challenges.*

Therefore, the responsibility lies with you to either swallow unhelpful assessments and have your self-esteem plummet, or to deflect the arrow, thereby refusing to be the target.

The power is yours.

We are all much larger than our fears and possess more might and strength than our inherent challenges.

HIDING OUR LIGHT

What happens when we hide our light and never fully display our capabilities?

Actually, we don't feel better for doing so.

We might feel resentful and jealous towards others who are capable of revealing their positive power, instead of seeing them as inspiration for the expression of our own abilities. We might hold ourselves back from new experiences and opportunities that would bring us joy.

In restraining our voices and life force, we deprive others of the gifts and wisdom which they could sorely need. There is nothing gained for anyone when, for whatever reason, a human spirit is prevented from expression.

Sometimes we might not want to be seen because we know that if we step up to the plate we actually might have to *do* something, and that 'doing' scares us no end. We might actually have to look into ourselves and see the transcendent light which came in with us when we entered the world.

Viewing our surroundings by that inner radiance is a lifelong quest that requires courage, trust and action. It also means we must have the humility to understand that we are human and are entitled to make mistakes. When we do not allow ourselves to be seen or to make mistakes, we risk the utter stagnation of our own being. It is only by pushing ourselves forward that we can be a part of the great flow that is fundamental to growth and life.

The real problem is that we don't feel large enough to step into our own potential. We don't yet feel ready to take on the unknown shape of a future self. It is satisfying to know where we are right now, but we need to muse upon how we might evolve for our future. Moving in incremental steps helps us get used to the idea of a possible new form so that we can begin to accept the fact that we are always more than we previously imagined.

Living in the midst of world convulsions composed of, among other things, health crises and societal breakdown is exactly where transformation is needed. Now is not the time to hide, but to expand and deliver that which is most positive for humanity.

You can only do so when you accept the fact that you are meant to be seen, listened to and supported. The fear of letting the world see you is detrimental to the very world that needs you. And it does need you.

You came into existence before you were even capable of having one thought about yourself. Something decided that you would make the trip.

You came to express something. You did not come here to excuse, deny or denigrate your worthiness or existence. Your purpose was to be. Therefore, judgment of your worth by others or yourself is totally ridiculous. Since you were made with intent, not carelessly, but with infinite thought and care, and given all that you might need to navigate the world, it is with reverence that you must accept this phenomenal gift of existence.

With that acceptance comes the knowledge that you are the keeper of the light, not only for yourself but for others. And what is more satisfying than to light the darkness for another? For in passing the torch, we illuminate the world.

5.

Conflict ... 'I want to, but I'm afraid'

*One of the greatest discoveries a man makes,
one of his great surprises, is to find he can
do what he was afraid he couldn't do.*

Henry Ford

Sometimes, we have a dream but are mortally afraid to go after it since we have experienced reactions from others such as: 'Why are you doing that?', 'that's not a moneymaker!', 'not a good fit for your personality', 'you have no talent', 'not smart enough', 'nobody in *our* family ever did that', 'who do you think you are?'

Sometimes, instead of the support you were expecting from others, like, 'Great, if that's what will make you happy, go ahead and try!' you instead have the experience of others trying to convince you of impossibilities, simply because *they* did not have the courage to try to fulfill their own dreams. It becomes too scary for them to support you emotionally when they were not able to do the same for themselves.

Sometimes people really have tried, but life circumstances did not permit the flowering of their dreams. However, at least they had the satisfaction of knowing they took action.

Sometimes jealousy of your ability to dream and create is what sadly makes people not wish to support you. Unfortunately, they don't realize that by supporting you they also allow themselves to uncover and give life to their own hopes.

You might also experience that finding success throws you out of the 'tribe'. Some people might feel threatened by the fact that you chose a different route than the one they were able to comfortably emotionally support.

Suddenly, your biggest supporters (if you were lucky enough to have them) could turn into slit-eyed, passive-aggressive dragons. Friendships can suffer, relationships may fray.

But is it worth it to let those relationships rule that cannot support your growth?

Usually, the conflict and fear we feel about going for our dream is in direct proportion to how important that desire is to us, but letting those less positive emotions rule can have huge consequences for our future.

Andrew, a lanky slow-smiling and kind guy, was considered a very gifted graphic artist at his college. Top of the class and possessing an impressive and eclectic portfolio, he had originally thought of applying for a graphic design position after graduation, something which would have given him the necessary business acumen towards his dream of leading his own graphic design business. After graduation, however, he found himself procrastinating time and time again in sending his portfolio to the very companies in which he was most interested.

As the months went on and the time lengthened away from his graduation day, he seemed to show less and less interest in pursuing his original idea and took a small job with a local printer in his neighborhood. His family and friends tried to understand his change of heart but never succeeded in getting a satisfactory answer to the seemingly sudden lack of enthusiasm.

Years went by and Andrew never did open his own business, but continued to apply his talents to local projects while neglecting his original intent to be in the spreads of glossy magazines with cutting-edge subjects as part of his own business. When I asked him about what had held him back from going ahead with his original goals, he replied, somewhat ruefully, that the thought of professional criticism of his work had been so emotionally frightening that he couldn't allow himself to even seek the very opportunities for which he had hoped.

In Andrew's case, nobody knows whether he absolutely would have been 'successful' according to his own definitions, but that is not the most important point. The fundamental mistake was in letting his fears overcome his desires, thus preventing him from traveling down a career path that probably would have brought him tremendous emotional satisfaction.

""

What would life be if we had no courage to attempt anything?

Vincent van Gogh

FOLLOW YOUR HEART'S WHISPERINGS

Whatever the difficulties, there is no reason why *you* should not give it a whirl. When we follow our heart's whisperings, we may end up in entirely different places from where we thought we were headed, only in hindsight realizing that indeed it was the most direct route to our happiness. And everybody ... even the naysayers, in some unknown way, will benefit from your courage.

There are ways to fulfill your desires which don't necessarily have to mean a full-time commitment if circumstances do not permit. Suppose you want to be a horticultural specialist ... a deep-sea diver, or an illustrator, but with three small children in tow you cannot, understandably, see your way to this opportunity. Just by partaking in a small fragment of your dream — through an internet class, lecture/presentation, book, conversation — you will begin to feel the excitement of movement, and to create, however unknown and ununderstood at present, small trajectories towards your larger goal.

It is not conflict or fear which is the deciding deterrent, but the decision to listen to them. Listen instead to your desires for they are the surest indication of who you really are.

> *It is not conflict or fear which is the deciding deterrent, but the decision to listen to them.*

""

*Everything you've ever wanted
is on the other side of fear.*

George Addair

6.
But what if I succeed?

We either make ourselves miserable
or we make ourselves strong. The
amount of work is the same.

Carlos Castaneda

Years ago, during a challenging time in her early twenties, Sheila noticed that while visiting her parents during a few days of vacation she began to have trouble navigating a certain staircase in their home. She would run up the stairs and then invariably feel hesitant and unsure, and trip over the top landing step.

After about a week of this, and wondering what was going on, it suddenly dawned on Sheila what was happening. She literally was afraid of taking the last step, the one that would bring her to the top of the staircase. When she figured out what it meant, she was amused and delighted that her mind had found such a beautiful metaphor for her fear of success and being 'afraid to get to the top'!

However, once she consciously decided to 'go to the top', running up the stairs and bounding past the last step was never a problem again.

So what happens when we actually do succeed?

Maybe you are the first one in your family to go to college or university, the first to break a traditional role in your circle of friends, or you just achieved your dream promotion, painted a masterpiece, got a starring role on Broadway, gave a fantastic corporate presentation. Congratulations!

And it is just at this point … when the doubts can start to slither forward … Are any of these thoughts familiar?

> 'It's a fluke I got this promotion, I can't do the job.'
> 'How will I ever do [fill in the blank] again, as well as what I've done already?'
> 'When people really find out about me they'll know I can't handle [fill in the blank].'
> 'How did I think I could *ever* do this?'

But of course, there are many reasons why we might have some of the thoughts above. For example:

> Self-doubt makes us feel that we don't have the abilities to handle what is expected.
> We are afraid that a change in our status will make other people jealous and cause disharmony.
> We feel that we don't deserve what we have received, even if we desperately want it!
> We can feel afraid of doing well, since even *more* might be expected of us.

Wow. What a lot of mind sludge to carry around after you've just tasted success.

In addition to negative thoughts, we sometimes self-sabotage our own success by doing something that will prevent us from moving forward.

Being consistently late to the Broadway rehearsals, not turning in assignments at school, missing meetings at your new dream job. There are a zillion ways to 'show' ourselves that we really 'can't' handle it.

COMPASSIONATE INVESTIGATION

Instead of wrapping ourselves up in turmoil and self-defeating behavior, we can choose instead to compassionately investigate why we are stuck in these negative mindsets in the first place.

One of the best ways I have found to get to the root of success fear is to ask the following questions, since fear may try to devour, but mind can always empower.

TO PONDER

> Why am I afraid to take this incredible opportunity?

> What negatives or positives might happen if I truly succeed?

> Am I afraid of further external expectations?

> What goals do I have for myself with this success?

To be afraid of success is only the fear of one's innate potential.

By going through this process and continuing down to the 'aha' moment where you discover what it is that you are truly afraid of, you develop a plan of action, geared towards future positive results. This is more productive than focusing on what you *think* is lacking within yourself, and concentrates instead on the positive aspects you bring to the table. To be afraid of success is only the fear of one's innate potential.

SUCCESS OR FAILURE?

When Julie was 35 she had a dream where after opening a drawer in a table, a huge beautiful green plant came spiraling out, shooting up into an enormous tree.

She was so frightened of this incredible fast change that she quickly stuffed the entire tree and plant back into the drawer. It was only later that she understood the meaning of the dream.

Realizing our potential and being scared by it is more common than people think, since it takes courage to be ourselves and to explore our dreams.

It is helpful to remember that real success is a lifelong journey. It isn't one particular point along the way, where you sit down in a blissed state and never do anything again.

'Success and failure' are simply how *you* feel about something in particular, but they have no intrinsic meaning in themselves. Sometimes a situation which seemed to be exactly what you were looking for can turn out to be a really horrible experience from a professional or personal standpoint. Was it a success or failure? It depends entirely on your point of view.

What we call successful or less-than-successful moments, brings us information about ourselves that propels us forward in our growth. It is up to us how we use that knowledge.

Exploring the above, we will feel much less fear upon reaching our goals, since the goal itself is but one stop on the way to somewhere else. Every 'success' and 'failure' is simply a step on the staircase of life. Sometimes we go up, and sometimes down. But does either direction constitute success or failure? It really depends on where you want to go!

To keep moving is the important action, since keeping our energy in transit in creative ways affords us continued opportunities, while at the same time offering possibilities for others as well.

Like a wonderful relay we pass forward the fruits of our creations to the next runner, so that they may go forth towards their goals!

7.

Great expectations: yours or others?

""

*You can't base your life on
other people's expectations.*

Stevie Wonder

Whose life are you living anyway?

When we are young we often hear, 'Oh you are so good at …
you should be a …' or 'Well, you really aren't very good at that, so
maybe you should do something else.' Sometimes, more directly,
we hear about someone else's choices for us: 'Well that isn't for
you … no one in our family ever did that.' Or 'I'm really counting
on you taking over the family business' etc.

It is very hard not to go with the flow of expectations from others, especially if they are loved ones who really do have your best interests at heart. Unfortunately, sometimes *your* heart interest is not what they consider to be in your best interests!

Many people follow the path of least resistance, only to find that they end up feeling miserable in what they have chosen, leading to unsuccessful careers and stilted creative outcomes with feelings of disappointment and lack of meaning. It's not uncommon to hear from my clients, 'I really wanted to do such and such, but my parents did not think it was an appropriate career for me and now I am stuck in something that pays the bills but which I detest.'

Unconscious expectations can also rise from *ourselves* when we feel we *must* follow a career path that someone in our family had previously tried to accomplish but did not manage to fulfill. We might feel we need to make up for *their* lost opportunities — a dangerous path, to be sure.

DREAMS FROM THE PAST

Bethany, sixteen, was the daughter of a talented dancer who had never, because of life events, been able to pursue her talents to the degree she wished. Although also a talented dancer, Bethany did not have the same passion for the art. Loving and respecting her mother, she dutifully worked through her grueling dance classes and took auditions, all the while feeling enormous pressure and expectation to pursue this as her professional career.

After a time of feeling immense conflict between her own career aspirations and the desire to please her mother, Bethany came to an emotional collision resulting in the decision not to dance professionally. It was extremely disappointing for her mother, but it liberated Bethany to enjoy dance from her own perspective while learning to support her own emotional rights concerning the direction of her life.

Questions may come up as to whether you *deserve* to make your *own* choices, especially if someone close to you was not lucky enough to have certain life choices. This can also cause inner conflict to the point where you might sabotage an excellent opportunity simply because a loved one never received the same good fortune or chances.

In the same way that you would not want your children to take on the darker aspects of your past, so must you not take on the shadow aspects of your ancestors or those whose lives might have been unfulfilled in some manner. It is not up to you to fix or be involved in a 'do-over' of other's lives, no matter how much you love them.

Sometimes we get stuck in feeling that because we have inherited a talent or opportunity we must use it or take it. But that is true only if it is something which our own heart desires. Every person deserves to create their own history and not simply to be a continuation of someone else's dreams.

People also think they should not allow creative dreams from their *own* past to surface in their daily lives. 'My husband/wife is working so hard, I really don't see how I can allow myself to take that class on architectural design just for fun!' or 'I know my wife hates hearing me practice, but I always wanted to have trumpet lessons!' When you allow yourself to express as many creative avenues as you need, you bring forth interconnected dimensions of yourself, leading to interesting paths for you and the people surrounding you. The more you engage with different aspects of yourself, the more engaging you will be to other people, which can lead to possibilities that never might have occurred otherwise.

In being true to yourself by listening to your own creative desires, you also encourage others around you to develop their own potential. People take their cues from each other — sometimes consciously, sometimes not. In expanding or narrowing your own boundaries you clarify to yourself and others what you expect from yourself, and what they can expect from you. The decision must come from the inside out, not the opposite. This gives you untold freedom to determine the course of your life, and lets others also have the same freedom in developing and expressing themselves.

There is not one correct way to live, despite what others would have us think.

TO PONDER

> How would I begin to think about my life if I were free from any expectations or influences from family, friends, teachers or professional colleagues?

> Because of the many advantages I was given by this person who was never able to fulfill *their* dream, am I trying to live a 'do-over' for them, or is this really my decision?

> What expectations about life have I accepted because of my fear of societal or religious reprisals, even though I am not in agreement with certain ways of thinking?

> Am I involved in [fill in the blank] because I need a sense of identity and wish to feel [strong, respected, powerful, in control] or be seen as [a high professional, in charge, the boss] or am I doing this for the opportunity to create something in a field I enjoy?

It might be helpful to ask others with whom you feel comfortable about their life stories, in order to understand how people have possibly held themselves back or, conversely, were able to break stereotypes and create different inspirational new life trajectories.

There is not one correct way to live, despite what others would have us think. The challenges and variables of life are a living kaleidoscope filled with changes of relationship, weather, personal situations, world events — all manner of positive and negative things. What works during one moment may not work in the next.

Because nothing is set in stone, our life maps may change daily, and intentions may shift as well.

Your only expectations should be those that are important for you, not as rules that must be strictly upheld, but as malleable and flexible vantage points which assist you in working towards a meaningful personal goal. Like taking a kayak through rapids, you paddle as best you can towards your goal while navigating the different currents in which you find yourself.

8.
How to love rejection

""

Success is not built on success.
It's built on failure. It's built on frustration.
Sometimes it's built on catastrophe.

Sumner Redstone

Been passed over for a promotion? Feeling lousy because you didn't win the audition? Had your manuscript rejected? Discriminated against because of age, sex? Your ideas laughed out of the boardroom meeting?

What is *wrong* with you?

Actually, nothing …

Every single one of us has had moments when our greatest wishes were just made impossible by someone else's decisions. Fairly or unfairly, the result was that you didn't receive the reaction you hoped would occur.

So what to do? Give up? Tell yourself all the reasons why it must be your fault? Or someone else's?

Or … look at the situation with a new eye and plunge into trying *smarter* to figure out how you are going to make the next time, or the time after that, the success that you are determined to receive.

People who have rarely experienced rejection in their life do not seem to have the same sense of confidence and self-esteem in the face of adversity as those who have learned through difficulties to cultivate persistence and determination. Some of the most successful people I know are those who have 'failed' quite a bit but nonetheless keep trudging on towards their vision.

KEEP GOING

Therefore, you *are* going to get there, but only if you keep going! Success is 80 per cent mindset and 20 per cent action, both of which are the magic keys to a desirable outcome. The mind, primed for success, will creatively tell you which actions to take. And if those don't lead right away to the exact scenario you were expecting, be assured that in some way, they are leading you in the right direction.

*Success is 80 per cent mindset
and 20 per cent action.*

Barbara, a charismatic, curly haired American actor, had many auditions in her life where the outcome was negative because of nerves, politics or the stars not being aligned. If she had decided, 'Well I'm just going to quit', there never would have been the incredible opportunities and life experiences she was fortunate to receive simply because she kept going and pursued every opportunity that presented itself despite the disappointments and horrible days.

After winning a certain audition in Europe, Barbara was thrilled! Everything was fantastic! The company wanted her, the director wanted her, the administration wanted her, and the country's unions definitely did *not* want her ... because she was a foreigner.

She returned, flabbergasted and crushed, to the United States and could have given up, except that she didn't ... she phoned and/or wrote every week for two years (!) to the manager of the company letting him know of her interest in accepting the position, and at the end of that time the unions and the company worked out a solution — and off she went!

That initial rejection (among others) helped Barbara to develop self-understanding and steely resolve, which turned out to be very important skills in her continuing career.

Rejections are often signposts that give you an indication as to some type of movement which needs to take place. I'm not saying it isn't painful. Acknowledge your emotions, and then choose (after a while) to give less attention to the situation by focusing on the next strategy which will lead you to success. Since everyone experiences rejection as surely as rain in the tropics, the question is how you will modify the blueprint of your emotions and actions to create a new vision of possibility.

Learn to love rejections as the subtle helpers that they are, in bringing you closer to what will be most valuable and enriching. Sometimes *not* getting what you wish may be one of the best things that can happen.

A hardworking and thoughtful young woman, Jennifer, who had lived in Paraguay for a number of years working with bright-eyed children in government-sponsored literacy programs, was in line for quite an interesting position in the international studies program at a small but well-known college. Prospects looked excellent that she would receive the offer, which included a great deal of student interaction, which she loved, as well as some international travel.

She very much wanted the position because of her lifelong interest and experience in international living and because she had the excitement and hope that her contributions would greatly benefit the students. At the very last moment, however, it appeared that this was not going to happen. Jennifer was extremely disappointed, since the position had held huge interest for her on many different levels.

A year later, however, she found out that, because of budgetary constraints and other difficulties, the position she had desired so fiercely had been eliminated. Fortunately for her, after not receiving that job offer she decided to move in a totally different direction, resulting in more expansive teaching opportunities and the ability to create and develop programs richly aligned with her core beliefs, both of which would not have been possible in the previously hoped-for position.

Winning or losing are only external constructs. The most important and helpful action is to be your best self in whatever direction you choose to move. In doing so, there is no competition, since no one can be you!

""

Rejection is merely a redirection;
a course correction to your destiny.

Bryant McGill

By focusing on being open and productive, magical scenarios will present themselves, even if you do not have the slightest idea what form they might take. Paths do appear, although it will require patience, as the universe has its own timetable. Very often we get extremely impatient that events are not happening as fast as we would like. But, as with anything that grows in life, there are stages which must unfold before the bloom. The constant stream of possibilities must recalibrate itself in order to transform into that which we desire, and action, patience and faith are the components which water our desires.

Therefore, you are not a product of what other people may think about you, but of what you think about yourself. Only you can determine who you really are, and what is of value to you, and it is vitally important to be supportive of that inner belief when the world believes otherwise.

9.
The challenge of change

""

Twenty years from now you will be more disappointed by the things you didn't do than by the ones you did. So throw off the bowlines, sail away from the safe harbor, catch the trade winds in your sails. Explore. Dream. Discover.

Mark Twain

What is it about the known that makes us feel so secure? Does the fact that we are comfortable with all the ins and outs of a situation absolutely mean that it is optimal for us? Perhaps we have been lulled into the false idea that change is always dangerous.

Even the expression 'the devil you know is better than the devil you don't' is a prime example of how we are taught to rationalize staying in a less-than-ideal situation, if that is where we happen to be. It is as if the unknown is always assumed to be worse, or inferior compared to what we are experiencing at present.

People sometimes stay in jobs, relationships and mindsets even when, for whatever reason, the expiration date is quite evident, hoping against hope that some miracle will happen to bring them into a new fulfilled reality.

But better realities are not *brought* to people. Circumstances come to meet us only as we take the first definite steps towards greeting them. It is a dance of trust and faith, and is certainly not easy. Staying in a negative situation, however, is far more stressful in the long run.

There are any number of reasons why we might feel afraid of change, some of which might be:

> loss of identity
> thoughts of not deserving something better
> perceived loss of control
> fear of upsetting others
> fear of the unknown.

Without change in our life, however, we would become extremely bored, as well as boring to others!

Change is a constant and starts before we are born. Our whole process of development and growth is change. Once we are here, our lives are filled with events and challenges that entail change (i.e. starting school for the first time, graduations, relationships, learning anything new).

Life *is* change.

However, when we become ensconced in a routine that makes us feel secure, we don't seem to like anything which may disrupt our false sense of security. As if repetition, like a mantra, could keep us safe.

Similar to a cat that always lands on its feet no matter which direction it jumps, we also must learn to have a flexible psyche in a world which guarantees us nothing *but* change. In doing so, we begin to understand that it is by taking risks, chances and opportunities that come our way that we remain the safest. We then open ourselves to a wider net of support and possibilities than we could imagine, and replenish our inner resources and creativity.

LEARNING TO EMBRACE CHANGE

How can we help ourselves to embrace change?

> *We can look back and see all the positive changes we have made so far.* After all, wherever we are now, in the best sense, is a result of previous actions which did not take place until we *chose* to take those new actions.

> *We learn by looking at the strengths that we do possess* and remembering how they were developed. Did we struggle through a difficult scenario and come out stronger afterwards because of our determination to solve a particular problem?

Even during the negative parts of our past we were honing ourselves for future success.

> *We can take small baby steps which will increase our confidence.* No one says you need to do the big, brave thing right off the bat. Learning to strengthen your 'change muscles' will give you the courage to make the necessary big decisions when the time comes. Find ways to make small changes in your daily life which will increase your feelings of bravery and self-reliance! After a while it will seem normal and natural.

> *Develop a support network.* Listening to people who only hold one point of view is not a balanced perspective from which to make a decision. People speak from their own experiences, *which are then filtered through their own emotions*. Therefore, their advice may be well-meant but might also be the *opposite* of what you truly need. In developing support, you may listen to opinions from both sides, but in the end, following your own intuitive wisdom usually produces the best outcomes.

> *Look for the constants in your life* that do not necessarily need to change. Not everything needs to change. As you move towards larger life decisions, rely on some of the constant and comforting aspects of your life that *are* a permanent fixture. People who emotionally support you, your own creative talents, skills and personality traits that have consistently helped you to navigate in the past.

*The future is only unknown until
you join hands with it.*

Once you make the leap into a major decision, do not look back and second-guess yourself. Whatever change you made was done because some part of you felt that it was imperative to do so, or you would not have done it! You can always adjust your course in the future, since *you* are in charge. The future is only unknown until you join hands with it. The first resolve should be to take some action, no matter how small, to begin the process. As the Cheshire Cat in Lewis Carroll's *Alice's Adventures in Wonderland* says, 'If you don't know where you are going, any road will take you there.'

PART 2: JUDGMENT AND CRITICISM

10.

Criticism: helpful or hurtful?

""

Don't be distracted by criticism.
Remember, the only taste of success some
people get is to take a bite out of you.

Zig Ziglar

Some years ago, I knew a young woman of impeccable character who was in the middle of deciding whether she wanted to apply to music school. She possessed a large enough talent to think about this competitive possibility but, because she did not know any of the teachers personally, she decided to have a trial lesson with one of the professors at a conservatory where she hoped to apply.

When I saw her again some weeks later, it was clear that the lesson had not gone as she had envisioned. She described a situation where the professor had admonished her severely and brutally about her hopes of having a music career, let alone entering *any* conservatory. She had received quite a tongue-lashing, resulting in the crushing of her hopes for a future performance career. All this from just one lesson!

Unfortunately, this happens more than you might think.

In the arts, business, other professions and scenarios, you will always find personalities who seem to relish breaking the spirits of those they encounter!

RECEIVING FEEDBACK FROM OTHERS

The next time you go looking for advice or critique on your performance and capabilities, whether in the office, on stage or in an art class, try to keep in mind the following thoughts, which might offer you some perspective about receiving feedback from others.

The person's background

Does this person have enough professional or knowledgeable background to make an appropriate judgment on your behalf? (Not just a higher position than you, but *real* expertise in your area?)

One of the most valuable pieces of advice I ever received from a college professor was 'Consider your sources'. Meaning, always consider the source of your information. What is the background of the person, their affiliations, belief systems, experience, education, etc.? If you don't know, or can't know all these points, at least try to find out some small details. The point of this is not to condemn or judge the person who is critiquing you, but to give *you* a better context to understand the reasons for their opinions.

Your best interests

If this person *is* qualified as a mentor, do they have your best interests at heart?

The answer to this question can easily be found in the manner in which the criticism is conveyed. If it is constructive, helpful and uplifting, giving you clear direction as to what can be improved in terms of reaching your goal, then yes.

On the other hand, if you receive a barrage of negative criticism without any obvious helpful path of action or emotional support, it can sometimes be a projection of previous disappointments that the giver has experienced themselves. This can show up as bitterness and frustration on their part, which is then expressed outwardly to others. Of course, there can be other very simple reasons as well. Sometimes a person just has an ego the size of a football field and believes they are the most valuable being on the planet, in which case I would go ask someone else for advice!

While some aspects of criticism may be very valuable, the way it is said, as stated, is incredibly important. And for a young person lacking life experience, it is of course especially detrimental to encounter someone who does not offer their opinion in a caring and respectful manner.

Dealing with negative criticism

When you are given 'negative' criticism, are you internalizing the 'negative' part of it, or using the applicable, helpful parts as a springboard for your future success?

Some people only hear the negative parts of what they are told, a situation which, when added to lack of self-confidence, then becomes destructive rather than constructive. Therefore, it is important to really listen to what is being said, to make sure you are not missing helpful information that could make a world of difference to you!

Success can be threatening to others

Unfortunately, for some people, your success is seen as threatening.

It's ugly but true. Sometimes the person in authority can be most jealous of the one seeking help, especially if they come with gifts that far outweigh the person in the mentoring position. Again, anyone who truly wishes to help you will do exactly that, by supporting your strengths and aiding the development of your potential.

There is another person who does have your best interests at heart but is not always capable of showing it.

You.

Consciously or unconsciously, we judge ourselves (usually negatively) way before someone else gives us their opinion. Then when something critical *is* said to us, it reinforces our own self-perceptions, leading to some rather uncomfortable moments.

Therefore, it is important to look at our own beliefs. To examine our backgrounds and 'consider the source' of our own thoughts about ourselves and others! You can only take the 'best' from judgment and criticism if it is a) given by someone who is truly interested in your wellbeing and b) accepted by you from a place of self-esteem and thoughtfulness.

""

Criticism, like rain, should be gentle enough to nourish
a man's growth without destroying his roots.

Frank A. Clark

11.

Guilt and potential

" "

Guilt is to the spirit,
what pain is to the body.

Elder Bednar

What stops people from being able to move forward, even though they ache to do so?

Of course, a lot of limiting reasons.

Among them can be a sense of guilt. A feeling that we do not deserve that which we very much desire. This is not always a conscious thought, for if it were, it would be that much easier to dig out.

So let's look at some of the ways in which we may unconsciously sabotage our dreams because of this sad little creature, guilt.

A SENSE OF RESPONSIBILITY

You might wish to pursue a dream someone else desperately wanted, but never had the chance to fulfill. Now *you* have the possibility, but feel conflicted and less deserving of it, because others were not able to manifest their previous hopes.

It is important to realize that dreams are individual, and as such need to be kept separate. Holding yourself back because someone else did not have an opportunity does not help you or them in the slightest! In fact, in this case, stopping the flow of creative energy is far more damaging since it now creates *two* situations where opportunity was thwarted.

In moving ahead into our own possibilities, and keeping our energetic flow, we might be able to give joy to another person by having them experience something through us that they might not have experienced otherwise.

Of course, to be *very* clear, this is not why we choose to go ahead. If we do, it is *because of our own desires*, not because it was someone else's dream or because we feel responsible for a do-over of someone else's life! This is an extremely important point to understand.

JEALOUSY

Your dreams are being fulfilled with ease and grace, but for someone else, it has been continuously difficult and burdensome to realize their goals. You might feel guilty because of the jealousy you feel from others.

Holding yourself back can cause you stagnation and resentment. By embracing your dreams, you can only inspire others to do the same! If some people feel negative emotions, that should not concern you, for in the final analysis your success can help others, whereas your guilt helps no one.

CHANGE OF FOCUS

You started in one direction but completely changed your focus despite the hopes, dreams and sacrifices of others to help you when you started out.

When speaking about life, sometimes the shortest distance between two points is *not* a straight line. Sometimes the meandering way brings us closer to our goals far more quickly and truthfully than the standard 'right way'.

To discover that we are on the wrong path, and to continue regardless of that fact, is one of the greatest mistakes we can make. We cannot lie to ourselves. Those who have helped in the beginning did so out of care and hope for us. To continue on the *wrong* track would not honor their material and energetic gifts. Being true to yourself allows what they have given you to flourish and spread roots further in the garden of your own hopes.

Far better to cut your losses and to start with a light heart and true purpose which will bring you faster and closer to that which releases your true potential. The turmoil of change is hugely preferable to permanent regret!

"

What a liberation to realize that
the 'voice in my head' is not who I am.
Who am I then? The one who sees that.

Eckhart Tolle

Maria is a young woman in her twenties who I consider to be one of the most successful people I know. Successful in different ways than you might think.

She is a gifted young painter who attended a prestigious art school with the dream of continuing her life as an artist. During her student years, she worked herself mercilessly to perfect her art, believing that if she just sacrificed herself physically and mentally she would be doing everything necessary for success and happiness. She was also driven by the fact that her family had sacrificed much to help her fulfill her goals.

Unfortunately, while she was at art school she experienced some extremely traumatic and damaging events which threw her life into a tailspin. Because of this, and several other events from her past, she developed substance addictions along with eating disorders.

With great courage, Maria decided to leave the school and enroll herself in a therapeutic program in another part of the country to deal with her overwhelming issues. Over a number of years she worked courageously to subdue the turmoil which had followed her for more than a decade. As a smart, strong willed, kind, sensitive, remarkably self-aware young woman she has huge drive and potential for anything she wishes to pursue. She may become a professional artist or not. It really doesn't matter. What does matter is the nourishment of her soul and her happiness in being a part of this world.

Her huge success comes from having lifted herself out of a tremendous ravine of despair and turbulence into a state of mind where she now knows she has a future of choices. She realizes that she controls her life, and no one else. It isn't easy. It's a battle every day. But there can be no guilt in making choices which are essential for our health and growth.

When we speak about potential, we remember that we are beings of many colors inside and out. We should also remember that there are many roads we can follow that can lead us to happiness and fulfillment. We may choose a path and then completely change direction if we so desire.

There are many roads we can follow that can lead us to happiness and fulfillment.

Although we do care deeply about the people in our life, and take into account how our choices will affect them, we must first be honest with ourselves, for only that clarity and self-understanding will bring the truest measure of health, contentment and joy for ourselves and the people we love.

12.
Standards of perfection

"

Perfection is man's ultimate illusion. It simply doesn't exist in the universe ... If you are a perfectionist, you are guaranteed to be a loser in whatever you do.

David D. Burns

Trying to do something with the *goal* of doing it absolutely perfectly will automatically kill the joy of whatever you are trying to accomplish! I'm not suggesting you shouldn't try your very best, since great satisfaction comes from accomplishment, along with confidence and joy of a challenge overcome.

Boredom arises if things are too easy. If we could accomplish everything perfectly with just a flick of our finger, we would be miserable!

When we say, 'Yes, I am a perfectionist' with a tiny smug smile, we have no idea of how much happier we could be if that weren't the case! Perfectionism is forever about reaching some unattainable goal. For whom? And why?

The problem with being a perfectionist is that it is a never-ending cycle of demands upon the self, which can be very emotionally tiring. Instead of enjoying the process of what you are doing and allowing a journey of discovery, the final result becomes the *only* focus.

This fear of not getting the anticipated result can be why people start but never finish projects. Sometimes they cannot even allow themselves to start for fear of making mistakes.

THE PATH TO DISSATISFACTION

The quest for perfectionism can lead to permanent dissatisfaction with ourselves as well as never-ending criticism of others. Trying to live up to an ideal which does not exist takes a great deal of pleasure out of living and can lead to unhealthy attitudes resulting in skewed ideas about life.

> *Having an all or nothing mentality.* If you don't become a star in your field you consider it a failure, instead of being happy about whatever success you *have* achieved, and the enjoyment and fulfillment of getting there.

> *Chasing after perfection* can sometimes make you feel more

shame, anxiety and diminished self-worth than others who are happily satisfied with simply doing the very best they can.

> *Believing that you can control the outside world* and make it perfect, so that you will have more inner peace and safety. Since we cannot control the outer world or make it perfect, this is a set-up for huge discomfort and anxiety. Controlling our inner world *will*, however, bring us the peace and safety we desire.

> *Feeling unlovable or worthless* unless you produce constant achievement. You believe that others' judgment of you is an important reflection of your own value, rather than realizing that simply existing is enough to merit being accepted and loved.

What it boils down to is that perfectionism is simply another type of fear. Sometimes we think that unless we are perfect we don't have the right to move forward or, heaven forbid, make mistakes. If we are not *the best*, then we have no right to be anything.

When you think about the Olympics and all the incredible athletes who train for *years* day in, day out, in the hopes of being considered the finest in the world, does it really mean something if one competitor wins by three thousandths of a point over another amazing competitor? Does it really make them the best in the world? Especially when they are being judged subjectively by other human beings? Is this not kind of crazy?

The dedication and wish to work hard and do the very best possible is admirable, but standing on the winner's podium and scowling at receiving the bronze or silver medal seems very strange! Something with their thinking, our thinking and the general inclination of society to place an emphasis on the fact that only perfection, only the gold medal is worth anything, is terribly misplaced.

There are qualities which are far more valuable than the gold medal, the crowd's adulation or the applause. I'm thinking of self-esteem, self-love, self-compassion and self-understanding. If that all sounds a bit selfish, perhaps a different perspective might be that if we internalized those aspects a bit more, it would be easier to radiate them towards others, becoming happier ourselves in the process.

Trying very hard to achieve your best is necessary for result and growth. What isn't necessary is the feeling that *if it isn't perfect ... it's nothing.*

This is unrealistic and destructive, and exactly where we sometimes find ourselves when we are in the process of creation. Unfortunately, in the case of the Olympic athletes or others who have worked with formative mentors, this attitude is often fueled by punitive authority figures who do not possess the heartfelt interest in the physical or emotional wellbeing of those they train, leaving their students with diminished self-esteem and lack of access to normal mirrors with accurate reflections.

BECOMING CURIOUS ABOUT YOURSELF

Curiosity can help us to discover if we might harbor some perfectionist tendencies.

TO PONDER

> Do you feel that you only have value by achieving successfully in the manner dictated by your family?

> Do you feel that you must know the answers to everything instead of being able to ask for help from others?

> Do you fear disapproval from others in general?

> Do you have a tendency to procrastinate when starting a major project?

When you become aware of the fact that you might be heading towards the slippery slope of perfectionism, you might find some of the following strategies helpful.

Try to break down a task into smaller chunks so that you don't let yourself become stuck at one particular point of the project. If one part does not work, move on to another. *Get used to movement versus stagnation.*

Allow yourself the 'luxury' of completing something at a level that may not match your usual standards, thereby proving to yourself that it can be done! *Learn to live 'imperfectly'.*

Understand that making mistakes is crucial to the creative process, for mistakes are simply signposts towards better solutions.

Be careful not to identify yourself with what you are doing. You are a human *being* first, and what you are *doing* is secondary. Therefore, again, compassion, kindness and self-acceptance are key.

Accept your flaws. Everyone has them. You are not alone! If you can accept this about yourself, you will find it easier not to rely on others' judgments to the degree that you do.

THE BENEFITS OF CURIOSITY

In cultivating an attitude of curiosity, rather than a fixation on the end result, our creative impulses, whether in the arts, the boardroom or the studio are set free without the rigid constraints of perfection. Our sense of fun, joy and anticipation bring us far more emotional satisfaction than if we are concerned by how we will be seen by others.

Curiosity is what helps us to confront the 'all or nothing' attitude which can travel with us on the path towards our goals. The ability to be inquisitive and curious in finding different routes towards our destinations, rather than doggedly sticking with one particular unhelpful way is necessary if we are to keep going when encountering the inevitable obstacles.

> *Curiosity is what helps us to confront the 'all or nothing' attitude which can travel with us on the path towards our goals.*

When my husband (who works with wood as a hobby) encounters a difficulty in a project, the first thing I usually hear are foreign swear words coming from the basement! Then all is quiet for a *long* time, and I *know* that he is actively searching for solutions to the frustrating problem. It may take him days or weeks, but the happiness that I see on his face from finding solutions more than makes up for the problem, and sometimes even gives him more satisfaction than the project itself!

Curiosity leads to creativity. Expending our energy on various solutions gives us the freedom to change directions in our thinking and actions, without locking ourselves into how something 'must' be done. This fluidity gives us much more emotional calm, knowing that we are not judging ourselves by a specific outcome done in a specific manner. In fact, we are not judging ourselves at all because we are having so much fun along the way.

As creatives, we produce for ourselves. Even if given a 'commission' to complete, it is still a work that springs from an interior creative impulse, which hopefully will mirror the desires of the recipient. The greatest masterpieces are realized when we do *not* think about perfection. When our minds are too busy being consumed with ideas and possibilities, and our days too filled with mistakes, as well as successes. Our prime objective, however, is in the expression of an inner impulse which cannot be denied, and comes to life aided by freedom from excessive judgment given by ourselves or others.

It might be the same as sailing a vessel. If you do not change with the wind, not only will you not go anywhere, but you could find yourself without a boat! The ability to sail with the circumstances is what makes a sail successful. It cannot be perfect, since there is no such thing. The sailing experience itself is the goal.

In thinking about perfection, which does not exist, we should remember that our greatest joy lies in the journey of our work.

The end result can be a thing of fascination, inspiration or beauty, but the spirit that created it is far more 'perfect' and magnificent than we can ever know.

13.

Performance and *you*

You are not here merely to make a living. You are here in order to enable the world to live more amply, with greater vision, with a finer spirit of hope and achievement. You are here to enrich the world, and you impoverish yourself if you forget the errand.

Woodrow Wilson

Why do you stand up in front of a group of people playing an instrument, giving a speech, spending hours at the canvas or pottery wheel, performing a dance, executing flips on a balance beam, writing your poetry in stolen moments, presenting ideas at work, working on preserving precious moments in a scrapbook or perfecting a fantastic routine on ice?

What is it that drives you to put in such an immense amount of energy and time?

Why do you spend days, weeks or years trying to perfect all that you will display? Well, here are some common reasons.

> You need applause and adulation from people to feel good.
> You love what you are doing and want to share it with others.
> You want to prove something to others, or yourself.
> You feel fantastic when you get to express yourself this way.
> You are doing it because others expect you to do it. Your family did it, your friends think you should be doing it.
> You really don't want to do it at all, but feel guilty if you don't.
> This is your identity, and without it you are not sure who you are.
> You need to prove to others that your creations have 'merit', otherwise you are wasting time and money.
> You are only doing it for the money.
> You like the constant charge of adrenaline that comes with doing it.
> You have to do it because of your job.

As you can see there are all sorts of good and not-so-good reasons why people spend so much of their lives involved in the practice of what they do. And with all of those reasons, good and bad, can come feelings of anxiety, fear, helplessness, lack of confidence and self-esteem because of the pressure of some kind of public performance or expected productive performance from others who do not see or understand the merit of what you are doing!

This is not just for performers on stage. Office-related anxiety and burnout is very real, as is the terror of public speaking and presentation or simply the emotional burden of justifying your creative actions to others.

Late hours of work, over-care and deadlines are all factors which influence how we feel. Home life also has performance pressure, especially with multiple roles as a parent, financial provider, partner or caretaker.

Performance is in every aspect of our lives since we all 'perform' continuously, in some way or another. Sometimes we might get the applause, promotion or favorable opinions we want so much, but we might just as easily lose a job or a relationship, or be looked down upon by others because of their ideas of how we should be, act, do, perform. Even when we think we are giving our best selves, we cannot control the way others think about us since everything we do is filtered through the emotions and judgments of the person viewing us.

This is why a committee looking to hire may have hugely personal and different opinions about a candidate. Their decisions may have nothing at all to do with the person applying and everything to do with their own personal backgrounds and ways of seeing life.

TAMING THE SELF-CREATED DRAGON

The good news is that when we experience fear and anxiety because we are afraid of how others will perceive us, we can begin to understand that *we* are in fact creating those feelings. Fear is not an external emotion determined to get in. It is a self-created dragon.

However, since we create our own emotions we can absolutely change our responses to difficult situations.

The reason fear and anxiety have such a hold on us in our performance and creative displays is that we have forgotten the reason why we are doing the performing or creating in the first place! It is first and foremost for ourselves. Our fears come when we give away our inner power to other people, by depending on their opinions to determine our own worth.

If we can keep our own sense of identity, then someone else's opinion would be and should be secondary. We will then realize that winning the audition or job is not the biggest thing in the world, but just a possible stepping stone in our life's blueprint.

> *Our fears come when we give away our inner power to other people, by depending on their opinions to determine our own worth.*

After conservatory graduation, I was accepted into the Grand Teton Music Festival for the summer, where all the participants were housed in gorgeous shared condominiums overlooking valleys of verdant green strewn with wildflowers, enjoying a backdrop of the majestic Tetons in the distance.

It really looked like something out of *The Sound of Music* — all that was missing was Julie Andrews singing and dancing her way through the meadows.

From our balcony in this magnificent valley, we could see about fifty cows dotting the lush landscape, softly mooing as they grazed.

One day I got the 'bright' idea to ask my roommate if I could try her French horn. I had never played a brass instrument before, so I picked it up, went out onto the balcony of our condominium, hoisted the horn and, taking the biggest breath I could manage, attempted to blow out what I hoped would be some beautiful, resonant sounds. Well, they certainly weren't beautiful, but I did manage some huge blaring bleats which traveled directly down into the valley.

In an instant, everything changed.

From a peacefully grazing, bucolic scene, mayhem ensued! Cows ran and loped in all directions, some bumping into each other in their attempt to get away from the alien sounds. Being a city girl, I had not even thought about such a possible reaction and, although it seemed very amusing at the time, apparently it wasn't *at all* amusing to the farmer who owned the herd ... as I later found out.

Even though at the time it was not a great moment for the cows (or the farmer!) I still remember today the incredible feeling of utter freedom, of just letting go, that I experienced in blasting my energy and excitement through that instrument out into the great beautiful valley and mountains. It felt like a joyous communion with myself and nature.

What a wonderful thing it would be if we felt this way in all of our creative endeavors. Letting our energy burst out to connect to ourselves and others, without causing undue chaos of course!

14.

The green-eyed monster

"

Comparison is the thief of joy.

Theodore Roosevelt

Jealousy … it seethes and hisses in its discomfort.

And yet, who has not experienced twinges in daily life, in our work, among our friends, in relationships? 'Why didn't I think of that?' 'Why them instead of me?' Why, why, why …

The boss who is envious of an employee and therefore tries to micromanage and control their actions. The hard-working double-shift mom who resents her more carefree friends. The workaholic colleague who complains incessantly about lack of promotions.

Feeling jealousy is not the worst part ... letting it eat you up alive is. But why do we feel jealousy?

Mostly it is because we do not trust ourselves or our capabilities enough to create our own possibilities. We are sometimes afraid to ask for what we really want, for fear of seeming needy, or weak, less knowledgeable or inadequate. However, being afraid to ask for what we need is exactly what will prevent us from moving ahead!

In the above examples, the boss could have maximized the creative output of her employee for the benefit of all, while at the same time gaining everyone's respect. The double-shift mom could have asked for help from her friends. The workaholic colleague could have faced his own fears and had an honest conversation with upper management. But fear prevented the best parts of each person from being exposed. Each case represents a situation where creativity was stifled because of fears about outside judgment.

Jealousy feels bad physically as well. Like a giant stopper in a drain, which permits no flow.

HOW TO DEAL WITH OUR JEALOUSY

The first thing to realize is that the aspect or situation about which we feel jealous might just be a smokescreen for other reasons and feelings we have not yet discovered.

Madelaine had grown up in a small, somewhat idyllic, rural town alongside neighbors who knew others' happinesses and woes. A comfy village where shared meals, accompanied by a side dish of goodhearted emotional comfort, were always available for those in need.

Most weekends, with great anticipation, Madelaine would go over to her busy neighbor who had a thriving ceramics business, and hop carefully but excitedly around the fiery, statuesquely placed kilns, waiting to see the beautifully transformed pots. The glazes and colors fascinated her, as well as the mystery of not ever knowing exactly how something would turn out! Over time, through the kindness of this neighbor/teacher, Madelaine learned to flow with the huge energy of the potter's wheel and to explore the possibilities in the magic and coolness of the wet clay. Her talent blossomed as her interest and skill grew, resulting in inquiries from people in and out of her area, asking about possible gifts for holidays and birthdays.

In her little town also lived two sisters who were both quite dramatically talented in drawing. Every show and competition they entered seemed to place them easily within the winner's circle, something which never happened for Madelaine because she never dared to enter herself as a contestant.

She felt rather jealous of their success but did not have the emotional courage to present herself in any sort of competitive situation. After a great deal of envy and bitter feelings, she decided to confide in her parents and a loving family friend. With their encouragement and wise counsel, Madelaine began to realize that it was herself and her own fears that were the greatest hinderance to her emotional freedom and creative potential.

She wasn't so much jealous of their abilities, she discovered, as she was of their capacity to express themselves without caring at all what others might think. Over time, Madelaine was able to rid herself of these worries and concentrate more on allowing the flow of her creativity to speak for itself. And now, years later, she has a reputation as a nationally respected and unusually imaginative ceramist who mentors aspiring artists of all ages, determined to instill in them the valuable lessons which she herself learned.

There are ways to disarm the beast of jealousy. The first is to realize that, at its root, envy suggests a dearth of self-esteem coupled with a lack of belief in one's own capabilities.

TO PONDER

Instead of resenting someone else's success, why not — just for an experiment — support their good fortune? Truly feel happiness for them. Encourage that mindset. See what it feels like to have a lighter emotion in your body. Feel the best part of your being start to expand. In doing so, you will notice over time that opportunities will flow more easily to you, as you learn that someone else's triumph is only proof that success is available to all!

By concentrating on your unique abilities, you will begin to feel your own strength and start to acquire the understanding that there is room for every single person in the world to have success.

To begrudge someone else's success is to believe that you cannot have it yourself. Whereas, by supporting others, you are basically saying that you have the capacity to receive 'your own' without taking from anyone else.

Creativity is not only that which you do in the world; it is very much how you *are* in the world. And how we *are* in the world determines our future.

"**"**

*A flower does not think of competing with
the flower next to it. It just blooms.*

Koshin Ogui

15.

Mistakes: the best way to success

> ""
>
> *I always go back to my grandmother's advice to me the first time I fell and hurt myself. She said to me, 'Honey, at least falling on your face is a forward movement.'*
>
> Pat Mitchell

What if we could go back in time?

To kindergarten, or primary school, where instead of feeling guilty and sad about mistakes, we learned from our teachers and family that mistakes were really okay, perhaps not comfortable, but really nothing to feel bad about. They were only happenings that didn't bring us where we wanted to go.

How nice if we had been taught that we could change things very quickly and try something else which might work better! And if we didn't understand something, even trying our hardest, it wasn't our fault. We just needed someone who had a bit more patience when they taught us, and really took the time to understand how we might think.

How differently we would feel about ourselves and the world!

Human nature being what it is, this is not what most of us have experienced. We have been taught, usually from a young age, to fear making mistakes *not because of the mistake itself* but because of the behavior it will elicit in others. Anger, threats, punishment and power plays can come from others while we sometimes feel fear, sadness, lowered self-esteem, anger and resentment. Not exactly conducive to helping us along the path to creative solutions in general.

Therefore, we must become the teachers and helpers that perhaps we never had. It's difficult but not impossible to replace the negative internal voices which have governed us for so long.

We tend to forget that they are just voices. And not *our* own voice. Not *our* own being.

External voices which give rise to anger and threats, because of our mistakes, usually come from those who have experienced the same reactions from others at some point in their lives. These individuals are terribly afraid to make any mistakes at all for fear that others will see them as weak or lacking.

In fact, it is the opposite. Those who can readily admit their mistakes are people with sufficient self-esteem who understand that a mistake is simply a mistake, and therefore they are willing to help others when they find themselves in the same boat. Those who cannot admit their mistakes are usually extremely insecure, and will not tolerate from themselves or others even a hint of dissension or lack of perfection. Therefore, who is a better role model? Those who are punitive, drama prone and intolerant? Or those who freely admit a mistake, thereby showing their strength and leadership? The former will never receive respect; the latter, always.

> *Those who can readily admit their mistakes are people with sufficient self-esteem who understand that a mistake is simply a mistake.*

Somewhere along the line, mistakes got a very bad reputation. As if they were creatures to be avoided at all costs. Something hideous to experience, especially in a professional situation. And yet they are a huge source of knowledge. If you don't make mistakes you cannot know the joy of reaching your highest success.

" "

*I make more mistakes than anyone else I know,
and sooner or later, I patent most of them.*

Thomas A. Edison

MISTAKES CAN FOSTER CREATIVITY
AND CONFIDENCE

Mistakes are what bring us to our greatest creativity! Sometimes doing something soooo wrong can lead to thought processes which throw open new doors of action and possibilities.

Some time ago, Jeff, a thoroughly engaging actor with an exuberant personality and infectious sense of humor, had thought of getting an MBA in arts administration, since he also had interests in developing arts programs with a sort of 'alternative' twist to them. He had gone through the lengthy process of applying to various graduate schools, experienced the joy of being accepted to his favorite, packed his bags and taken off … and within weeks felt utterly miserable, understanding what an incredibly wrong decision it had been for him.

After a few weeks of torpid despair, so unlike his usual sunny personality, he had a conversation with one of his former mentors, where he laid out his conflicting desires concerning future possibilities. On the one hand, he wanted to act; on the other he wanted to create educational programs in the arts. After several hours of hashing out future scenarios, Jeff was invited by his mentor to be a teaching assistant at a summer program in California. It was during that experience that Jeff surprisingly discovered a love of teaching, and all the incredibly interesting challenges of helping someone else on a path of discovery.

The experience that had been gifted to Jeff came in exceedingly handy when he eventually opened his own studio helping actors and others handle the unique aspects of a career in the public eye. Therefore, out of his own turmoil came an experience so perfectly suited to what he does now. A mistake transformed into an epiphany. He might never have discovered it if he had not gone through that miserable process.

Mistakes also make us more confident (after you recover from possibly feeling awful), since if you have mortally screwed up, things can only improve after you take positive actions! The important thing is not the mistake itself, but what it will teach you in terms of moving forward (and faster) in the direction you want to go. The more mistakes you make, the more you realize how they are just bits of information which can point you in the right direction. You also learn just how resilient and resourceful you can be. These qualities cannot be accessed when everything is handed to you on a silver platter, since real resilience is learned by picking yourself up from the dirt when things go wrong, and forging on ahead.

"

Mistakes are the portals of discovery.

James Joyce

Using up emotional energy by berating ourselves for imperfect actions is a colossal waste of time. A little kindness towards ourselves in terms of our own learning process does wonders for our self-esteem and capacity to move on. And if we are able to do this for ourselves, then we can also give others the same respect, kindness and consideration that they need and deserve. A win for everyone.

16.

When in doubt ...

*One of the ego's favorite paths of
resistance is to fill you with doubt.*

Ram Dass

Doubt sometimes feels as if we are being crammed into a small uncomfortable box, wondering how we got there and how we will get out. In a real sense that is what is happening!

The psychological box we are sitting in is much too small for its contents.

Our gigantic, amazing selves contain all the tools that are needed for any situation. Unfortunately, we don't always know that. We doubt our abilities, strengths, innate wisdom, capabilities and all the other gifts which come packaged in our unique beings.

Just to be clear, it is not bad to have *some* self-doubt. It is extremely reasonable at times to question our assumptions. Self-doubt may help us to more clearly analyze a situation in order to reach deeper understanding and better results. Usually this does not happen when we 'know' all the answers.

However, when self-doubt consistently prevents us from taking action, it is no longer a wise friend but a gnawing emotion that stops us from moving forward. Self-doubt dilutes our energies, saps our creativity and, along with indecision, can literally give us a feeling of weakness. Very often this manifests as a lack of energy and ongoing fatigue, almost as if there existed a battle within ourselves concerning our inherent abilities to handle important issues.

Fear of making mistakes or not being in control also masquerades as self-doubt. When we never take action because we are afraid to fail, or are fearful of mistakes, we avoid risk. Or so we think. But there is a huge risk. By not pushing the boundaries of our own capabilities, we miss the chance of living the most emotionally rich life possible.

Sometimes self-doubt is an unconscious indicator that we really don't want to do a certain action but have not yet admitted it to ourselves.

Jody, a software engineer, was offered a lucrative and stimulating position located in a company on the other side of the country from where she lived. It fulfilled all her interests and dreams, but nevertheless she consistently spoke of her anxiety about handling the requirements of the new job. In reality, it certainly had nothing to do with her abilities, since she graduated first in her college class and had many admiring recommendations from colleagues and former employers. After much discussion and introspection, she realized that she did not wish to leave her home and the area where most of her family and friends lived. Her self-doubt was merely a ruse to shield her true thoughts from herself. Thoughts she felt she was not entitled to have because of the 'fantastic opportunity' the job offered.

We might also find ourselves trying to explain away our self-doubt as a result of something related to past factors, such as our families, teachers or long ago experiences. Sometimes, unfortunately, there can be an addiction to our past struggles and self-doubt, keeping us in a loop whereby we constantly take action from a somewhat wounded place. While these factors may indeed be contributors, we must always remember the incredible power that lies within us. The power to determine our own thoughts.

We all want to get rid of something and gain something else. Fear/courage, poverty/wealth. But we cannot hold two things at the same time in our consciousness. In order to have courage we need to release fear and self-doubt. The universe will not give you something unless you make a real place for it!

> *We must always remember the incredible power that lies within us. The power to determine our own thoughts.*

All of us have had negative experiences in the past which *unconsciously* shaped our attitudes; however, the wonderful thing is that we can *consciously* reshape our attitudes. When we do that, we might find that our reactions to the same set of circumstances will be completely different than those we previously experienced.

A CHANGE IN ATTITUDE

Suppose you need to give an important presentation to a group of people in a highly influential sphere. Speaking in public may never have been your strong point, but this time the circumstances might be such that it must be done. Instead of being terrorized by fear, self-doubt, what-ifs and other doomsday scenarios, because of internal discomforts or past experiences, you could decide to revise your attitude. After all, the only difference between you and someone else who has no fear of public speaking is *not* capability, but attitude. Here's how you can help shift your attitude.

Play a game

Way before the expected event, go back in your mind to past public speaking experiences (for example) that may have been less than wonderful, and imagine that they went differently. Revise them into the experiences you wish you'd had. And feel the difference this makes. Revel in these 'new' past successes and bathe in how good this feels. Soak these wonderful feelings into your body and sit with them day after day, feeling the confidence and enjoyment from the success of those previous experiences.

As you acclimatize yourself to these new feelings, you'll begin to feel much more confident and actually begin to look forward to what you can share with your future audience. After all, you are bringing them new information and ways of thinking!

This exercise will go a long way towards conditioning your mind for desired outcomes. There is no reason why your presentations should not be the way you wish or the way you imagine.

Talk to yourself

It is also helpful to have a sit-down with yourself, as if talking to someone else. By feeling empathy and understanding for the 'other person's' fear and self-doubt, you'll very often come upon insights which freely bubble to the surface. In other words, by trying to help 'someone else' you can bypass your own mental obstacles and allow your creativity and inspiration to flourish.

How important is it really?

Another way to handle self-doubt is to decide how important it is to you. Is the goal you are working towards more important than the self-doubt? Or are you so conditioned to feeling this emotion that it becomes stronger than the thing you most desire? In other words, how badly do you want to reach your goal? Our wishes and our self-doubt cannot be equal, since one is always stronger than the other.

In order to give self-doubt a little less weight, it helps to develop an attitude that allows for the possibility of *multiple different* outcomes in a situation. Like a chemistry experiment with a surprise outcome, go with the flow and accept the variable results that occur as part of life, and not as a judgment of your own self-worth.

TO PONDER

> If I were writing an article about my personality strengths, what would I say?

> What do I say to others when they are filled with doubt?

> Can I make a list of actions I have done which show my capabilities in past difficult situations? For example, 'I helped a sick person through a tough time', 'I handled a financial crisis', 'I dealt with difficult people', 'I conquered my fear of [fill in the blank]'.

Everything counts, since life is full of situations that require our attention. When you sit down and account for all the complex situations you may have encountered, you begin to understand that there is a great deal more to you than you may have thought.

17.

Stage fright: halls and eyeballs

" "

Failure feelings — fear, anxiety, lack of self-confidence — do not spring from some heavenly oracle. They are not written in the stars. They are not holy gospel. Nor are they intimations of a set and decided fate which means that failure is decreed and decided. They originate from your own mind.

Maxwell Maltz

Once upon a time, in a château in the south of France, I was slated to perform in an evening summer concert as part of a music festival in one of the château's magnificent chambers. Several of us had been in the Provence area for a few days, to rehearse at the castle during the evenings when the public was not present.

During those long, royal blue summer evenings it was completely still at the château, as if the owners were very late in being driven back by the footmen in golden carriages, with no sounds of their tired horses unevenly clip-clopping on the front cobblestones. Soft summer breezes wafted the fragrance of lavender, and outer rampart walls remained comfortably warm from the intense afternoon sun.

Inside, huge, magnificent paintings of haughty, bejeweled ancient aristocrats stared down their pointed noses at whomever dared to be in the room, while the crystals in chandeliers twittered and twinkled with even the gentlest of steps upon the parquet floors.

It was in this space filled with ghosts, past, present and future, that I would perform a rather difficult work for the townspeople and attendant officials. It was an important occasion for a multitude of reasons having to do with Franco-American exchange and other niceties.

Preparation had been great for this concert — perfecting technical challenges, memorizing the music and looking forward to a piece I truly enjoyed. Nevertheless, I was terrified, not least because one of the most renowned violinists in the world, who lived in France at the time, was going to be there.

Minutes before the concert I sweated and shivered, feeling absolutely as if my instrument had become an alien being.

As I made my way down a small number of stone steps leading to the improvised stage, I slipped on the worn polished middle one, smoothed like ice by centuries of feet, and came crashing to a halt at the bottom. Fortunately, I had the presence of mind to yank my arm into the air, thereby preventing my violin from being completely smashed.

I was so shocked by what had occurred and the fact that I still *had* a violin, that all fear completely left me. After a mind-numbing stunned moment or two, I made my way out to the stage ... and scored a completely happy performance.

I learned three things from this blowout experience.

First, I would *never* again wear such ridiculously high heels, which had looked so beautiful in the store; second, that my fear was literally all in my mind, since it disappeared completely when a large shock replaced it; and third, that arnica really does work for colorful, painful bruises on one's rear.

WHY DO WE GET SO ANXIOUS?

Performance anxiety. Two words which themselves can cause nervousness.

Why do we have it? Let me count the whys. Fear of:

> being seen
> feelings of shame in not living up to self-expectations or others' standards
> criticism and judgment
> showing lack of confidence
> success
> failure

> forgetting what we want to say or perform
> turning into a blubbering idiot.

But there are also more subtle things that can contribute to our feelings of stage fright.

Much performance anxiety is based on the untrue perception that we are only worthy if — and only if — we receive positive judgment from an audience. However, I believe that the fundamental reality is quite opposite.

I believe that the public's role is to *witness* creativity as a catalyst to unleashing their own (perhaps stifled) creative impulses. Whose heart has not been gladdened by a street performer, whatever they do? The fact that they are out there demonstrating their innovative sparks always intrigues and makes us eager to watch.

People may come to see something, to unconsciously experience a facet of themselves that has not been explored. We are fascinated by skill because another person is playing out a part of ourselves, an alternative path that we haven't consciously chosen.

When they don't 'do well', they spoil our fantasies of living that particular moment. By harshly judging the performer, we are at the same time judging and shutting off parts of ourselves since the performer represents unaccessed self-potentials. The performer can sometimes sense this judgment as a 'do or die' situation for themselves if their whole identity is wrapped up in external acceptance. This then causes them anxiety, sadness and a lowering of self-esteem.

WHAT TO DO?

The most successful ingredient to battle stage fright is to take the emphasis away from the audience.

How to do that?

By not performing 'for' an audience. What I mean by that is that despite being on stage and performing *in front* of an audience, the primary person that you are creating for should be *yourself*.

But isn't that selfish? Aren't we all here to 'share' with the audience?

Yes, you are sharing with the audience, by dint of them being allowed to *witness* what it is that you do. You are not necessarily there to *give* to the audience.

When an audience pays for a ticket, they are paying for an *experience* that they would ordinarily not have. They hope to see, hear, sense, understand something which usual life does not provide.

The performer, on the other hand, spends their days finetuning this experience to their own satisfaction since it brings them huge psychological harmony. Only after that is it then shared with others, only after having been worked through the performer's being. However, this intense work is not, and should not be, with the audience in mind.

The audience becomes transfixed by the results of the performer, because they can finally experience a small portion of a different reality, which they do not have on a day-to-day basis.

When you are able to separate yourself psychologically from the audience and its reactions, you are able to more deeply access the magical parts of yourself, bringing to the fore even more than you realized. In those deeply felt moments of performance, you are not even aware of the audience, not even aware of yourself, and at that point the audience and you become one on a much more profound and magical level. A level at which there is no judgment of any kind, good or bad, since it has become a unity of understanding.

When you worry about the audience, you have already divorced yourself from your own creative power.

When you plumb your own depths, you bring the audience with you to that sacred point.

This is why it is so important to think of yourself first, and secondarily, if at all, of the audience.

> *When you plumb your own depths, you bring the audience with you to that sacred point.*

But what about auditions? Nobody judging me is interested in my 'sacred points' or 'unity of understanding'.

To a certain extent this is true, and also not true. If you can maintain your center and experience *yourself* at your most profound, there is no doubt that others will be drawn into your experience as well. What your listeners *do* with that experience is out of your control, since in most cases auditions are based on extremely subjective (and political) perspectives.

The most important thing as a performer, or a creative person of any sort, is to be your own self. You will find as time goes on that you will become more accepted precisely because of your originality. Negative people will be heard only as tiny echoes from the past, squabbling in the dust.

All of the reasons for stage fright or lack of self-confidence can be vaporized when the emphasis is taken off the audience or external mutterings and brought back to the most important person in the world at that moment ...

Yourself.

Not in a judgmental way, but in the freeing sense of going on a wonderful trip with everything you need and realizing, as you take in the incredible views, that the journey, the vistas, the self, your exploration, are all one.

All of your efforts come to fruition and allow you to experience a total immersion and identification with that which you are creating. This wonderful feeling is not based on external judgments of your creation, but on the release and flow of the life energy which created it.

And *that* is what the audience comes to see.

PART 3: SUCCESS IN DIFFERENT GUISES

18.

What is success?

" "

*Whether you think you can
or think you can't, you're right.*

Henry Ford

Success is what we think. Literally. If we believe we are successful even though we only have $20 to our name, then we are! No amount of money, fame or power can make us feel successful unless we decide in our own being that it is so. Because in actuality there is no such thing as success or failure.

One person's 'success' can be another person's 'failure'. For somebody on a diet, it is a success not to eat that one last piece of cake; for someone trying to gain weight it can be seen as a failure not to finish it.

Success, in terms of reaching *our* goals, is the result of right thinking and right action. Easy to say! But what is right thinking or right action? To begin with, right thinking is thinking in ways that create a real blueprint for your vision. You wouldn't start building a house without a design, so why treat your goals as less worthy of a plan? It also means never allowing yourself the *indulgence* of swallowing internal or external negative influences. It requires that you continuously do the best actions possible, in order to keep pushing on towards your goals. And lastly, it means you can never, ever, give up until you get to where you want to go!

Nobody said it is easy. It takes huge motivation, mental discipline and determination. But it is within our power as human beings to accomplish anything (within reason!) that we seriously want to do in life.

That is not to say you will not encounter difficulties along the way.

It's almost a cliché, but nevertheless true, to say that the bigger the vision, the more we can assume there will be bumps and lumps along the way. However, the most common pitfall occurs when we encounter a big obstacle and *assume* it is going to stop us. It might do so temporarily, but, like a rock appearing in the middle of our path, if we continue on, despite any bruises and scratches we might receive in scrambling over it, there is sure to be a continuance of path and possibility. Perseverance is the number one reason a thorny situation *can* usually be resolved. And lack of that same quality will usually give us an opposite result.

Suzanne was a very articulate and charming mother of two young children, which meant a very busy schedule on top of her

English teaching position with a local school. She loved her work but harbored a secret desire to continue her education by obtaining a Masters degree in Communications. Under the circumstances it would have seemed impossible to do such a thing: with two rambunctious children, tests to grade and attempting to have quality time with her husband, who also worked full-time.

However, anyone who hung around Suzanne knew she was not the sort of person to be deterred! She started small and, by earning extra money tutoring children after school (while her own children played nearby in the classroom), she was able to take courses piecemeal towards her goal. It took her eleven years to receive her degree, culminating in a huge party thrown by her friends. But today Suzanne has a position as a public relations manager in a local theater company and couldn't be happier. Not only that, it afforded her children the lesson of seeing how a goal can be reached even through difficulties and the passage of time.

Success, most importantly, is not necessarily acquiring possessions, having money, fortune, power or fluttering off to another country. It can be those things, but only if they are the tools which allow a *furtherance* of a vision. This creates the happiness we all seek, for without vision, hopes and goals to inspire us, we stagnate like growling ogres forever ferociously guarding our small hordes of gold but doing nothing with them.

Society has rather rigid definitions of success, but success in any measure is that which makes our hearts sing. Is it not success to bring a smile to a care-filled person or to inspire and give support to someone facing obstacles?

Not too long ago, I gave an informal one-hour presentation to a group of young dancers in their early teens who were in between their various classes and other events. Looking at their young and shining faces it was lovely to see them listening intently as we spoke about *their* important dreams, visions and future possibilities. Somehow, whether it was an alignment of the moon and the stars or something else, at this particular event a meeting of the hearts was manifested and all felt our energy as one.

At the end, several of them came up to offer me warm hugs, which were happily received. The experience was so delightful with these young people that I fairly floated out into the beautiful evening sun beginning to set over the summer fields outside the studio. It would be difficult to not consider this experience an absolutely sterling success on many levels and, although I may never hear from any of them again, the evening was a wonderful gift.

> *Success, like love, lies in the eye of the beholder.*

Success can be found everywhere, in small and large moments. It can be found in the mirror when we look and see someone with whom we are at peace, therefore able to honor ourselves, and our inborn gifts while having compassion for our faults. Success, like love, lies in the eye of the beholder.

No matter who you are, yesterday is gone, and only in the present moment lies your destiny.

If the past harvest was bitter, know that the season is over. If it was abundant, enjoy the sweet fruits and save the seeds for your future. Plant only that which will flourish in the soil of right thinking!

19.
Confidence confirmed

""

Confidence comes not from always being
right, but from not fearing to be wrong.

Peter T. McIntyre

Confidence. Such a comfy word. Something full of plump feathers ready to support you in whatever position you find yourself. It's not something some people have more of than others. It's something that some people can *access* more than others. We are all born with it.

If we didn't have it, we wouldn't be able to get up in the morning to do anything. We have confidence that we can make ourselves a cup of coffee and do the necessary things that will allow us to be productive.

So why when it comes to learning or doing something new, does our confidence put out its front paws and come to a screeching halt?

Sometimes we have been told, in one way or another, that we can only be good at a certain number of things and no more. As if there is a boundary we cannot cross! If we are wonderful speakers we cannot be good designers. If we are analytical and data driven, we cannot be artistic. If we are artistic, we cannot be businesspeople. And on the stereotypes go, round and round.

Of course, many of these pronouncements travel with us from a very young age: 'John is the quiet one.' But when we've outgrown our younger selves, who is there to tell us, 'Wow John is such a fantastic public speaker — such charisma!'

We are made up of many sides, many visions, many roads, although we may choose to only travel a few in our lifetimes.

So, what is confidence? The Oxford Dictionary defines it thus: 'Confidence is the feeling that you can trust, believe in, and be sure about the abilities or good qualities of someone or something.'

In my mind and experience, confidence is also the ability to go into a situation and feel that you will not be afraid of the consequences if things don't go as you planned. In other words, you know that you will still be alive and kicking even when you haven't managed to do your best. It might hurt from your ego's point of view, but whatever happens you know that there will be other opportunities and that you will be able to learn from the experience.

If I were going into the jungle with a guide, I would have much more confidence in the person who is sure in their ability to get us *out* of any negative situation, rather than a guide who is absolutely confident we will never encounter difficult situations in the first place!

In our daily lives of board meetings, difficult collegial communications, frustrating rehearsals, less-than-stellar presentations, unplanned irritants, along with adverse news and events, we need to develop ways to handle the turbulence of our own existence. To do this, we need to access our innate confidence and know that we can handle whatever comes our way, whether an unplanned stage debut, a deadline of yesterday for a business project, an uncomfortable but necessary meeting or being unceremoniously shoved forward by life to do something uncomfortable.

We all have the capability of dealing with most curveballs. If not, we would have been eaten by wild animals long ago.

> *We are made up of many sides, many visions, many roads, although we may choose to only travel a few in our lifetimes.*

HOW DO YOU DO IT?

So, how to be confident when we need to be?

Practice!

No matter what it is you need to do — public speaking, presentations, handling difficult people — the best way is to do it over and over again until it becomes an organic part of you, not something that you stick on yourself from the outside. When you are able to do that, you will enjoy both what you do and the results, along with the natural confidence that comes when your inner core is undisturbed.

Take some risks

Try things that are outside your comfort zone. I'm not saying you should immediately go rock climbing, but even doing things that make you a tiny bit fearful will enlarge your horizons and point to capabilities you had no idea you possessed. The first time I learned to paddle a canoe in deep waters, I spent much more time in the water than the boat, owing to my inexperience and terror. But it got better, and I became much less afraid.

Think about playing more and winning less

As children, we play for the sheer fun of doing so, learning in the process how to constantly arrive at new solutions and even new rules. Somehow as adults we lose this spirited ability to let our minds freestyle into new ways of thinking. In our quest to 'be successful' we forget that there are many different ways to arrive at a goal, and that very often a half-baked thought that we think is awful can lead to a fantastic idea.

Act as the person you would like to be

Sometimes, taking on the qualities of the kind of person we would like to be helps us to get there faster. How does that person walk, talk, handle situations? What kinds of thoughts do they think? And what types of thoughts do they think about themselves?

As a music student, Jacob was once was put in the position of having to do a performance in quite a large, prestigious concert hall in New York on very short notice. Although he had practiced as well as he could for the event, he still felt incredibly unprepared. It didn't feel like a concert, but more like some bad dream where he would go on stage and not have the slightest idea what he was supposed to be doing. Fortunately, in reality it wasn't quite that bad, but to him, it felt awfully close!

His pianist, a wise and experienced woman, said some very comforting words to him just before he sailed out to the stage. 'Sometimes Jacob, you just have to go on, whether you are ready or not.' For some reason when she said that, it immediately took off the incredible pressure Jacob had set up for himself with this performance. He just imagined himself as someone who was ready, with an attitude that all would go well. And it did ...

He had put on, like a jacket, a successful 'persona' and that, plus the best preparation he could do at the time, carried him through. In other words, he had acted the part and his abilities were released. Kind of magic, but it worked!

When you learn to stretch and enlarge your confidence in different ways, it then begins to more easily fit situations where you might need a little boost. Kind of like a muscle. The more you strengthen it, the easier it will be to pick up heavier objects when you suddenly have the need.

" "

No one can make you feel inferior
without your consent.

Eleanor Roosevelt

20.
A case of 'mistaken identity'

""

Life isn't about finding yourself.
Life is about creating yourself.

George Bernard Shaw

Maybe there is more than one you! At least we know there is more than one possibility of you, more than one choice of who you are and how you decide to live your life.

We spend a lot of time thinking ourselves into how we will conduct our lives. We choose majors in our education, we wonder about what jobs will further our passions or simply pay for them.

With our myriad possibilities, we can vlog from exotic destinations, create online courses from home while eyeing our children, paint in our corner studios, dream up the next 3D printing possibilities or livestream all night long. Truly, there is an abundance of possible creative avenues. And when we have found something that inspires us, we do it. Usually for a long time.

And this is good, since it gives us an opportunity to become better at whatever it is we are doing.

The problem comes when we begin to identify solely with whatever we are doing, to the extent that we don't know who we are without it. That can be a frightening prospect. Who are you if you are suddenly escorted out of the building and don't manage 500 employees any more? Who are you if you can't dance, sing, perform for the non-existent public because of a public health crisis? Who are you if funding dries up and you are unable to continue your scientific research? Who are you if you are at home with one eye on your toddler, and the other on your computer screen?

WHO AM I?

This is a question that reverberates throughout life, regardless of what one does to earn a living. Usually we try *really* hard to ignore the query because if we don't have a concrete label that *we* feel comfortable with, it feels very daunting to answer someone else's questions about our identity.

We try to hold on to our titles, jobs, relationships (even sometimes negative ones) as though we cannot survive without them. But we can. We survived before they came into our life, and we will survive as they pass through and away, changing into other possibilities.

> *We try to hold on to our titles, jobs, relationships (even sometimes negative ones) as though we cannot survive without them. But we can.*

Positive identities can also trap us. If you are known to yourself and others as a successful businessperson, artist, doting parent or sports star, and some cataclysmic change occurs in the world that prevents you from doing your thing ... who are you?

That is precisely what Gabriel tried to find out about himself when he took twelve months off from his ice-skating career. It wasn't easy, after spending an entire life up until that point in constant preparation for competitions. In fact, it was terrifying. But he badly wanted to know who lived behind this identity of a 'professional sportsman'. During that year he stayed off the ice, didn't perform and did a whole lot of different jobs that had nothing to do with his skating.

'The scariest thing at the time,' he said, 'was *not* not doing my profession; it was in realizing how awful I felt without an identifying label. And experiencing how other people instantly pigeonholed me if I didn't match up with their preconceptions of who I was, and where I ought to be at my stage of life.'

So, he continued, 'I decided to toss that extremely annoying, external, judgmental thinking away into a box marked "Not Applicable".'

As it turned out, Gabriel experienced a great deal about himself in that year. He got acquainted with other strengths that he possessed, and learned (and was surprised at) how he reacted to happenings in completely different situations than the ones in which he usually found himself. He understood that there was a huge world out there which could not care less about his profession or him. In fact, it was really freeing to learn that nobody, except his family and friends, cared about him at all!

While his ego *may* have taken a slight hit, it was an incredible feeling for Gabriel to know that indeed there was someone else there besides the 'professional skater'. A person who enjoyed discovering new interests that probably would not have been encountered otherwise.

We can become so used to wearing the same clothes for years at a time that we forget there may be other clothes to choose from. Sometimes it's good to throw our identities in the washing machine and put on something else for a bit, just to see how it feels, and discover what other ideas and parts of ourselves may surprisingly show up!

Life is changing so ferociously fast at present, that who you were yesterday or even today might change completely by tomorrow.

And while that might feel extremely challenging, it may not necessarily be a bad thing, even if not very comfortable at the moment. On the plus side, it certainly shakes us out of our usual ways of thinking.

We love our routines and stability, our small nests and secure habits, yet sometimes in the great Ka-Boom of change we find positive qualities within ourselves that we would never have experienced had it not been for the tsunami of movement forced upon us.

So perhaps we are not who we thought we were, or at least not the completely finished person we imagined. And that's really quite okay. For, like the phoenix rising from the ashes, we can begin to soar in ways we never thought possible when we realize that we are the ones who determine our flights.

21.
Playtime

""

Necessity may be the mother of invention,
but play is certainly the father.

Roger von Oech

Do you remember, perhaps, the wonderful feeling of being surrounded by different colored blocks on the floor?

Everybody let you sit by yourself and have fun with your toys. Your mind was loose, bright and curious! No thoughts of a mortgage, to-do lists, dry cleaning, grocery shopping. The only things that captivated your attention were the possibilities in all the shapes at your disposal.

Sometimes you knocked things over on purpose and started again, while time flowed or even stopped. You didn't think about it because, for you, there was no time! There was only being in the moment and exploring your world.

Wouldn't it be great in our lives if we were encouraged to play as much as we are urged to work? To think about potentials, instead of constant results.

It *is* really imperative to do that.

Especially in our busiest times with a million things to do, it is incredibly beneficial to schedule short minutes of mind relaxation. By that I mean moments that allow your subconscious to stretch, expand and see the daylight.

By engaging in activities which have no external goal, we often experience some of our most creative ideas. It is not for nothing that many people get their best ideas in the shower or while washing dishes. When we do an activity that is somewhat set on automatic, our subconscious mind is free to wander, with the results of those meanderings often bubbling up to the surface.

A TREASURE TROVE

It is a very different feeling when we wrack our brains, going round and round to find an answer to a problem.

When we are consciously working towards a goal, we use only the information and memories we have in our upstairs library (the brain), but when we 'let go' we find access to a much larger trove of information.

Where is it? No one has any idea. We only know that it exists and that it can be accessed. When we do access it, we often come up with ideas that are perfect answers to the problems at hand.

And usually quite elegant solutions at that!

So, playtime is not useless, 'wasted' time. It is a time where the subconscious gets a chance to deliver ideas because we are in receptive mode rather than action mode.

Ideas very often surface *between* thoughts. Almost as if they try to dart in before you can slam the entry shut with a conscious thought. Some of the best 'aha' moments seem to appear unexpectedly, like a cat, who comes from nowhere and darts in the door the second you open it! For sure it wasn't there a moment ago, but it's there now!

Play comes from experiencing something needless … without a reason to do it except to have fun. Fun improves relationships not only with others but with ourselves, allowing us to relax out of our identifiable selves and labels to explore something different.

> *Play comes from experiencing something needless … without a reason to do it except to have fun.*

Play also recharges us, improves our memory and releases stress. Finding something that makes you lose track of time, even on very busy days, is a 'recess' from which you will reap lasting benefits. Much more than if you continuously keep your nose to the grindstone.

JUST MESSING AROUND

It has always been amusing to me when someone has created something lovely — a drawing, a poem, etc. — that their typical response after a compliment will be, 'Oh, I was just messing around,' as if they need to excuse themselves in some way for not producing something 'serious'. Or as if the creation has less merit because it was conceived during moments of relaxation.

Must all of our creative endeavors come to life only through suffering and hardship?

Of course, work is necessary in any creative endeavor, but the 'play' and exploratory aspects of the work are what keep us fresh and buoyant, able to access new ideas. Play is the wind which helps to sail all creative vessels.

The interplay between that which we know, that which we do not and the ability to put disparate ideas together is what fuels creation. To access that state we need to once again sit on the floor of our being and play with possibilities without constraint or judgment from ourselves. It is a delightful feeling we would do well to recapture since it leads not only to mental refreshment but also a deeper dialogue with ourselves.

"

We don't stop playing because we grow old;
we grow old because we stop playing.

George Bernard Shaw

22.
The beauty of gratitude

" "

As we express our gratitude, we must never forget that the highest appreciation is not to utter words but to live by them.

John F. Kennedy

So many things to be grateful for. So many things we take for granted.

When we are children we simply live and enjoy our own being. And this is right. We come and explore the great playground of life, tinker with all the exquisite variables and laugh with delight when we have discovered something new for ourselves. It is this wonderment and constant reaffirmation of the miraculous that children bring to 'grown-ups'. As we teach them to navigate their existence, they teach us, once again, to appreciate the world we have all come to visit.

In later years, we might think we learn about gratefulness from comparison. When we hear about something terrible that that has happened, we feel lucky that we have not experienced it.

But that is not gratitude, that is thankfulness. We are thankful that we have not experienced the terrible things we read about. Thankful that some outside act or occurrence has not befallen us or, conversely, thankful that someone has done something wonderful for us.

But true gratitude is the act of appreciating what you *already* have, versus what you would like to have. It is an acknowledgement of that which you already possess. Our ability to walk, talk, hear, see, feel, taste are indeed miracles which most of the time we take for granted. Our senses to enjoy the world have been given to us as the most unbelievable gifts.

We must be grateful! Every day of our lives we can learn, must learn, to enjoy the exquisiteness of the moment.

This morning I woke up and saw our pine trees absolutely glistening and sparkling in the sunlight, filled with luxurious, heavy water droplets from the previous night's rain. The lushness of the tree was adorned by hundreds of colors from the piercing sunbeams. How fortunate I was to be greeted in this manner!

But, like all of us, I do not walk in bliss all the time. I grumble about traffic, taxes and all the other rumbles and tumbles of life.

Yet, since I have been fortunate to work with and help so many different kinds of people, I have come to realize how most of us carry our fears and burdens from place to place, never realizing that in fact we can lay them down.

We can lay them down on the banks of gratitude and think about the good things that we carry.

Once when getting an eye check-up, the light they used was so bright that I actually did not see out of one eye for about 10 seconds. Nothing, just blackness. I was horrified, and very calmly (with the utmost inner panic) said to the doctor that I couldn't see anything at all. He replied that I would see normally very soon. When I did, the comparison was so immense, and my relief so intense, that since that moment I have never again taken my sight for granted. It is a pity I needed that minor experience to have gratitude for my sight, but at least I did learn.

When we fill ourselves with gratitude, we can literally feel the abundance bursting forth. Again, it is the feeling, not the words, which concern us. When your body feels gratitude, it is a most nourishing sensation which, happily, is entirely under our control to experience!

GRATITUDE AND CREATIVITY

You might be wondering, what does gratitude have to do with creativity and success?

Just about everything.

When we concentrate on that which we have, we hold feelings of abundance in our bodies and minds. We become what we feel.

If we are billionaires yet consistently feel poor, then in our minds and bodies there is no difference between us and those who truly have very little. Therefore, what good are our billions if we *feel* impoverished?

> *When we concentrate on that which we have,*
> *we hold feelings of abundance in our bodies*
> *and minds. We become what we feel.*

We will only attract a certain result in the outer world as we have the capacity to experience it in ourselves. For this is the only way we will recognize it when it arrives. By definition, the word 'recognize' means to identify (someone or something) from having encountered them before; to know again. We must have the knowledge of that thing or person previously within ourselves in order to 'know it again'.

To do that we train ourselves to experience it from within before we seek it from outer sources. That training includes holding feelings of gratitude for what we have, no matter at what level, which enables us to consistently tap into the energy of abundance and success.

A desired result is like a foreign language. Unless we have the capacity to understand what is being said, it doesn't matter how many times someone might repeat something to us. The understanding has to be in yourself first, in order to be able to comprehend what is being offered to you.

If we are consistently focused on lack, then that is what we shall experience. For in the very act of wanting more, we are already broadcasting that we do not have enough. Instead, we should be constantly focused on what we *do* have, since that attracts a completely different energy.

Like attracts like.

Gratitude is an acknowledgment that we already 'have'.

Living with, and by, those feelings is how to bring peace to the turmoil in our hearts, minds and bodies. It is not some syrupy sweet emotion that we force ourselves to have because we have been told we must. It is one of the most powerful emotions that we possess, and as such can liberate us from places of despair, ruts into which we have fallen and confusion as to our place in the vistas of the unknown. Gratitude is an acknowledgement of our greatness, and the greatness of all that is.

TO PONDER

> What *are* the things I am profoundly grateful for in my life?

> Are they just thoughts, or can I physically incorporate this gratitude in my body?

> Can I feel this gratitude as a foundation upon which I build my future desires?

23. Creativity and dollars

> " "
>
> *The purpose of life is to discover your gift.*
> *The work of life is to develop it. The meaning*
> *of life is to give your gift away.*
>
> David Viscott

No pain, no gain is what most of us have been taught since the beginning. Whether it is hoisting weights at the gym or slaving away late at night, it is ingrained in us that there is no reward unless you suffer.

As if we need to *suffer* for everything before we are entitled to anything nice.

But hold on! That is absolute nonsense!

The best things in life come from a place of mental freedom, emotional lightness and flow. It most certainly means that work is involved. The definition of work, however, does not contain the word suffering!

In the best sense, our work is that which encourages us to stretch in our creativity and service. Without work, our lives have no purpose, or direction. And by work, I do not mean only the type of work that receives a paycheck. Disciplined work, preparing our minds and bodies for a task, even if difficult, can always be enjoyable even though some parts may be less 'fun' than others.

Our society measures our success by how *it* defines success. It certainly does not care what the individual in question thinks about him or herself. But to really live and enjoy our lives, how can we constantly allow ourselves to be bound by the definitions of others?

It comes back to our fear of being expelled from society, out of our tribe, when we dare to create our own definitions. Society, however, can of course be enriched by different ways of thinking.

In regimes of oppression, this is much too threatening. As a result, the arts (and creativity in general) are the first to be suppressed. It is well known how 'dangerous' free expression is to authoritarian rule. Oppressive regimes fully recognize the power of creativity and how influential it is over minds, to the obvious detriment of those who wish to control how people think.

> *To really live and enjoy our lives, how can we constantly allow ourselves to be bound by the definitions of others?*

We should be careful not to become authoritarians in our own lives, by denying our creative impulses because of our fears that:

> - we are not good enough (good enough for what?)
> - don't deserve to be paid (as opposed to?)
> - we are not deserving of recognition (from ourselves?)
> - we might be wasting time (instead of?).

Our society draws clear lines between those it deems as creatives and all others. Why does this dichotomy exist? The following small story illustrates this psychological divide.

Once, after a performance in a foreign city, we had an after-concert reception in a very lovely embassy, where indoor fountains created wonderful mist for the plants cleverly arranged around the basins. Fluted, thin crystalline glasses were filled for us and the local VIP business personnel, with something resembling sparkling wine.

Sounds ideal, yes?

Actually, it was far from it! We were all incredibly hungry after the performance and needed some real sustenance, which was nowhere to be found. Alcohol plus lack of food does not help a performer's stomach, mood nor ability to stay sober!

Along with the fountains situated in gilded, chandeliered rooms filled with stiff, uncomfortable horsehair sofas, was a group of about 50 of the aforementioned local business community, a good portion of whom spoke some English, as did most of the performers.

One might have thought there would be some interaction between the two groups. After all it *was* a meet and greet! I did my best to engage in conversation with some of them, but soon realized that they were absolutely terrified of speaking to any 'creative types'. It all began to resemble a third-grade dance where everyone was petrified to cross the room for a dancing partner. Despite the fact that we were all human beings, it was just 'too scary' (as one of them told me) to talk to anyone who was so different from their world. 'One was allowed to enjoy it, but not to partake in it.' Very sad.

In our Western society, it is rarely acknowledged that 'serious' professions and 'softer' creative abilities can go hand in hand. Stereotypes abound of the tortured, suffering, imbalanced artist who doesn't know a thing about their bank accounts, or the businessperson who scoffs at the notion of the CEO privately taking a watercolor painting class.

However, like all silly stereotypes, we find that most very successful professional people allow themselves to access their creative sides, not only following their intuition as trusted counsel in difficult situations but learning to extract and reassemble information from many different sources. This kind of mental cross-pollination is exactly what makes their success possible.

Our society rewards icons and stars who we are encouraged to adore. Singers and sports celebrities, among others, are permitted to earn millions of dollars. We have no problem with this, since we are meant to support and identify with them. Somehow, though, we do not give ourselves the same admiration when we attempt to express our inner visions through the arts, business, design, science, etc. Is the amount that we are paid, or not paid, a true representation of our inner selves? I think not.

Since the beginning of time, humans have yearned to express themselves. We give ourselves very little support because we are 'not professionals' or 'it's nothing compared to ...'. But why compare? Why isn't the expression of what we do enough to merit our own support? Children happily show us their drawings, without the least bit of concern about whether they are 'good', expecting that we will proudly put them up on our refrigerators.

But with ourselves we say, 'Well, what I am doing is not like so and so.' But does it have to be, to be worthwhile? Do we need the adoration of millions of people to give ourselves permission to explore our interests? Can we call ourselves an artist, speaker, writer, business creator, healer, sports person, if we never are paid a dime for it? Indeed, are you worth anything creatively if you haven't received payment for your creations?

Society allows us to be creative within certain confines, very selectively within our jobs or when we are needed in some way. We are allowed to take time off for illness (barely!) but not for self-expanding moments of creation. The shortsightedness of this is that business needs brains that are flexible, analytical and daring enough to be able to transform vast amounts of information into new forms. This can only come with training of the mind and spirit, coming from the constant movement of our thoughts into new combinations of ideas. As has been spoken about in recent years, the future of business in general will be dependent on our right-brained creative gifts.

It's rather like the wide barrel of a cement truck, which must always turn so that the cement does not harden into rigid forms! Our thinking processes must do the same. By constant exploration of new ideas and experiences, we will prevent ourselves from hardening into old modes of thought.

The day when people are sent home to figure out knitting patterns (for example) instead of always thinking of the 'bottom line' will be a day when the new grooves configured in their brains by this exercise may beautifully solve a problem at work. The more varied information you possess on different subjects, the greater your creativity will be.

Before there were professional art schools, there were creative people. The famous cave paintings of our ancestors were not painted by those with degrees from art academies, nor was ancient pottery discovered in archeological digs necessarily done by the most skilled artisans of their time. The simple desire to create is what has lasted from one civilization to the next. A record of humankind's hopes and dreams, a cataloging of day-to-day experiences. Messages from the past created in quiet, reflective moments.

It is necessary, if we are interested, to hone our skills as best we can so that we are able to express more succinctly what lies within us. But even without that interest, the desire to create, no matter how small, should be nurtured, since even the smallest tributary eventually flows further to a larger river. Opportunities in life come by doing, creating and experiencing. One never knows where something will lead.

Creativity is powerful, demanding and vital. We need it in times of calm and in times of chaos. We need it for our mental health. We need it to help solve the world's myriad problems. We need it to remind us of the glorious possibilities that exist within ourselves, and we must use it without fail to forge powerful and positive futures if we are to remain a viable and thriving civilization.

> *Opportunities in life come by doing, creating and experiencing. One never knows where something will lead.*

24.

Aligning yourself with success

" "

I can't change the direction of the wind, but I can adjust my sails to always reach my destination.

Jimmy Dean

The world is in turmoil. It has always been in turmoil and probably will continue to be so. Unfortunately, this seems to be the only way positive change *eventually* occurs. However, we need to remember that in the middle of chaos, no matter how difficult, we can still have success. In our lives, communities, countries and world.

It is crucial to take sustenance from our previous successes if we wish to retain the motivation and spark necessary to find solutions to our and the world's problems. It takes creativity, determination and a fierce desire to move forward despite the raging emotional, biological and physical fires of our planet.

Therefore, we must start in our own lives. We must learn to align with our successful visions for change, which should include the success of others. Our success does not depend on subjugating others but rather on helping everyone to develop their creative potential.

BUT WHAT DOES IT MEAN TO ALIGN?

Part of the definition for alignment means to bring into cooperation or agreement a particular group, party, cause, etc. This means that we need to keep ourselves immersed in the very essence of what success is. We need to be in constant resonance with its energy.

If we go into a job interview, audition, performance, meeting or almost anything in life that requires our participation or creative juices, and we do not carry the *idea* that whatever we are going to do will have a positive outcome, then it probably will not happen.

Aligning with success means that we expect there will be a positive result of some sort connected with our actions. We must feel that success in our bodies as if it has already occurred. We must connect with, and live, the emotions we would feel. We must talk, act, move, make decisions based on the 'fact' of our success. And if it doesn't turn out to be the exact scenario that we wanted, we need to know that, whatever it is, it is *still* on the way to success.

Because it can be no other way.

When you align with success, you are aligning with an outcome that might take myriad forms. Forms which you may not have anticipated, forms which may be greater than you could have imagined. You are aligning with an energy, *not a specific result*. That is very important to remember.

> *When you align with success, you are aligning with an outcome that might take myriad forms.*

When Robert, a rather captivating speaker with a wonderfully dry wit, was preparing for an important speech he was to give at a university conference, he decided to work on his way of *thinking* about this event with the same degree of thoroughness that he used for the factual part of his presentation. During the crucial months ahead of the event, he did not consider that there was any possibility other than success. 'I pretty much brainwashed or "mind washed" myself,' he said.

It was not easy for him to do. It took a considerable amount of mental effort to accomplish this state of mind. He had to deal with all the usual fears and doubts that we all encounter. But since he wanted the result, he decided to put in the required mental preparation as well.

Finally, on the day of the event, a few minutes before the talk, one of his friends, who had come to offer 'support', asked him what he would do if things did not go as well as he hoped! Not great timing for a question like that!

But nevertheless, Robert's mental training had been so strong that he honestly could not even understand the question. The question literally did not compute. It did not make sense within the mental framework that Robert had constructed over the many months. He gave his friend a quizzical look and proceeded onto the podium, where he soon had the audience in stitches.

I hasten to add that the important part of this story is not that Robert made the audience adore him, but that he was able to present at the top of his abilities because of his previous mind work. For whatever reason, his best appealed very much to his audience. The actual success, however, was that his mind allowed him to bring forth his true potential.

Which brings me to the subject of affirmations.

AFFIRMATIONS

Affirmations are great, if you believe them.

The question is *how* one goes about believing. Is it a mental decision divorced from emotion or an integrated body decision based on feeling and emotion? In my personal experience, it is the latter.

Affirmations only come to fruition when they are imbued with life force, which is you.

What I mean by that is, if you simply repeat day after day that you are going to receive the job of your dreams, you will be repeating affirmations for a long, long time.

However, if you involve your entire body in the affirmation and actually *feel* in your body what it is like to have that dream job, what emotions you have, how you relate to the people there, where you live, what you wear and any other positive, solid feelings you can conjure up, then real belief becomes not merely an intellectual exercise but a full-bodied experience.

It is precisely those emotions and feelings which will magnetize opportunities and alert you to needed actions, leading to the desired result. It doesn't mean you sit back in an armchair and wait for the results to drop like a cherry into your lap. You still need to take all the positive actions that you can towards your goals.

The Latin word for emotion is 'emotere', literally meaning *energy in motion*. In our case, our belief and trust are the energies that we put into motion (our actions), inevitably leading to the realization of our dreams. Most people do one or the other, not realizing that like a chemical experiment you need both ingredients to produce a transformation!

When we truly believe in something, that trust, whether in a person or situation, is unshakable. It is the foundation that makes all further actions possible. Aligning with this trust, and belief, is precisely what aligning with success means. Transformation starts in the mind and body. From the inside out!

25.
Your success pocket

""

We don't see things the way they are.
We see them the way we are.

Talmudic saying

It's so easy to remember all our bad mistakes. So easy to dwell on things that went wrong. So easy to be angry at ourselves.

But what about our good points? Our successes? Where we made a difference in someone else's life? So easy to forget, so easy to disparage and say, 'Oh, that was nothing.'

When we do that, however, it sends a message to ourselves

that our achievements in general are really not worth very much, and therefore that *we* are not worth very much. This attitude is not helpful for our self-esteem or the furtherance of our goals. If we cannot enjoy the sights along a journey, why bother to go in the first place?

Celebrating everything we have been able to accomplish is very important. From learning our first steps, signing our name, conquering Photoshop or learning to fly an airplane, everything we accomplish is worthy of our feeling good about ourselves.

> *If we cannot enjoy the sights along a journey, why bother to go in the first place?*

It is a very interesting and worthwhile exercise to write a list of 100 things you have learned or accomplished in your life. Everything counts as success! From learning the alphabet, getting your driver's license to learning how not to have someone push your buttons. You will be amazed at your accomplishments!

But how easily we take all those successes for granted. Only the 'failures' stand out, looming down upon us like dark clouds, rarely allowing us to pay attention to the sunny days. Perhaps it is because we may be a tiny bit afraid of our success. Success means others notice.

Sometimes people are jealous of our success because, in comparison, they think they are 'behind' in some way. However, keeping ourselves down because we are afraid of other people's jealousy or other reactions is not good for anyone. Certainly not good for us, when we should be enjoying the fruits of our labors, and not good for others, for whom success should be an inspiration.

CREATE YOUR OWN CONTAINER

Be that as it may, remembering our successes is a very balancing way of dealing with our less-than-successful endeavors.

That is why I create a special container for myself. Instead of throwing away or conveniently forgetting about all the things that I have done well, I put them into a mental 'Success Pocket'. This pocket goes with me everywhere and is quite handy for those moments in a stressful situation where I might have spectacularly bombed!

It's not that I forget about it or ignore it when I have done something which is less than stellar; it's that I remember all the other things I *have* done extremely well. It doesn't mean I don't try to learn from my mistakes; it means that I recalibrate and remember that I am not perfect (and don't need to be), thereby skipping over the self-recrimination and judgment phase to the more helpful aspects of analysis and continuance of action.

It's really quite draining to always be down on ourselves and ready to pounce on our slightest missteps. There are many people in the world who are *so* ready to do this for us; therefore, we absolutely have no need to take on that mission!

Success breeds success. Successful people never operate from a 'victim' status. We should expect to receive good fortune. We need to learn to be good receivers, otherwise how can we expect others to receive what we offer them in terms of our creativity and gifts?

We need to prepare the container to receive what we wish. That means learning to resonate with our past achievements so we are able to feel the energy of success as a constant hum in our beings. Feeling our success is not arrogance — it is an acknowledgment of directed action that has reached its goal. Knowing this, and tuning in to our success, enables us to continue pursuing that which is important to us and expands our power to be of service to others.

And really, when it comes down to it, that is what we are here to do. No matter how we wish to live our lives in terms of our personal interests, it all arrives at what we can do for others. How can we use our creativity to make that beautiful blue marble in space a more balanced and thriving world?

We can do it if we are in balance within ourselves, noticing our faults as guides to make adjustments, while at the same time reveling in our successes. We cannot help others to reach their potential if we are not cognizant of our own.

> *We need to learn to be good receivers, otherwise how can we expect others to receive what we offer them in terms of our creativity and gifts?*

The more successful you are, the more vitality, energy and connection to source you have available. Being resonant with success is like connecting to an electric socket: if you aren't plugged in, you can't turn on the possibilities!

This is why success is important, not because it might bring fame, money or other material things, but because it pulls more possibilities out of you for the world, and conversely from the world to you. A never-ending cycle of creativity and positive influence. So develop your success pocket. Make it bottomless and able to hold all your most beautiful treasures. You never know when something in it might be the perfect thing to help someone else!

26.
Success comes from the whole you

"

Who looks outside, dreams;
who looks inside, awakes.

Carl Jung

Very often we think of success as coming from one talent that we
may have, or some specific actions we have taken towards a goal.
Although this can be true, it is not the entire picture.

We tend to forget, or perhaps did not know, that it is our entire
being with all of its perceived positive and negative facets that
enables us to accomplish what we set out to do, and not just a
slice of ourselves containing specific abilities.

Working from the wholeness of our being supports us when we are going through a rough patch. Very often we tend to become myopic and focus intently on just the specific problem we are facing, whether a relationship, mathematics problem, public presentation or a better way to slice bread. While that is necessary, of course, it is also important to approach the task from a feeling of totality, not just our brain, eyes and hands.

To make an analogy, it is very much like playing an instrument. People tend to think it is all happening 'somewhere out there' in front of them. Something to do with the instrument, their hands, the music. And yes, those aspects are important, but it is also necessary to realize there is an entire part they have forgotten. The rest of them!

Their backs, legs, neck, feet, waist, torso also have physical feelings. The rhythm and the music are created and displayed by the entire body working together to produce a physical sound. Added to this are the beautiful emotional components of mind and heart, bringing a spiritual meaning to the listener.

Music, as an example, is delivered through a system of interdependent pathways resulting in something that another being can enjoy (even gorillas and elephants, apparently!). It is amazing and inspirational to experience a performance where someone is playing from the 'roundness' of their being.

And so it is with success. When we approach a creative project, we draw upon our minds to set the framework, steps and strategies we will use. But there is another equally important thing we need to do.

This action consists of soaking our whole being in the vision of the end result. This vision is not something we watch like a movie.

It is more that we are *in* the movie, acting as the main character, feeling all the emotions we would have in our perfect scenario, behaving as we would in the fulfillment of our vision and doing this from a sense of peace and confidence in our complete selves.

Usually, though, there is a strong tendency to identify with only slivers of ourselves. Slivers, in this sense, meaning very narrow and specific parts of ourselves. However, we are not only our talent, business sense, artistic prowess, intellectual or curious natures, but everything we have ever experienced, including our past failures and successes, personality quirks and temperament.

> *We need to live from an acceptance of totality, which means surrendering to the completeness of who we are.*

Therefore, to predicate any one result based upon a small portion of our psyche, whether that is an inborn talent or simply a desire for a certain outcome, is not enough. We need to live from an acceptance of totality, which means surrendering to the completeness of who we are, our strengths as well as our perceived weaknesses.

When we do this, we work from a body and soul that have vastly more amounts of information and collective wisdom for us to draw upon, allowing us a much better chance to succeed at what we wish to achieve.

We must also ignore the constructs that society has set up for us about timelines or variables concerning age, race, gender, location, education, etc. While society has its own 'rules' concerning these categories, 'deciding' what we can and cannot do, they are rules we do not have to follow at all on our own creative journeys.

Remembering who we really are allows a profound strength to rise in us like springtime sap, displacing the energy of fear and past negative experience and replacing them with a deep sense of comfort and trust. When we live from our power and not from our wounds, we become unassailable and unstoppable.

We are amalgamations of all that we have been, coupled with a deep desire to fulfill our potential. The point at which these two energies touch can and does produce magical results, blending like watercolors into infinite states of possibility. This can only happen when we allow ourselves to surrender to life from a state of self- acceptance.

Accepting all our facets, including our successes, 'failures', belief systems and doubts, along with our positive and negative experiences, is the nourishment we need for our creative futures, compassionately allowing us to discover new worlds within ourselves. Worlds which are created from the fusion of *all* our myriad parts.

PART 4: WRAPPING IT UP FOR COSMIC SEND-OFF

27.
Trust in … whatever!

*The inability to open up to hope is
what blocks trust, and blocked trust is
the reason for blighted dreams.*

Elizabeth Gilbert

Sometimes when you don't have any control over a situation you just have to trust that things will be okay.

I had contracted food poisoning the first night I was in Russia, practically ruining the entire trip for me and my husband. I remembered that the orange juice at a friend's house had tasted strange, but at the time I thought it was just 'Russian' orange juice.

It was … It was Russian orange juice that had been sitting on the counter non-refrigerated for a couple of days. In any case, leaving out the very gory details, I staggered around for the three weeks we were there, losing weight in the process since I had no desire to eat, and in the last week, on top of everything else, I developed a whopping cold. On our way back to the airport, we drove in something resembling a taxi that went, without exaggeration, at least 100 miles an hour.

That car practically drove on two wheels, scattering chickens violently into the air as we passed through villages, nearly mowing down several elderly ladies who were sweeping the streets. Sitting in the back seat with my fever, and clogged nostrils, without the slightest ounce of fear (which under normal circumstances would have been at maximum level) I simply gave up. I surrendered and threw my being to the winds of the almighty, with a tiny hope that we would make it to the airport alive.

Arriving at last, we made it to our flight, landing later in Paris for a layover where, to this day, I remember exactly what step of the escalator I was on when my fever broke and I became mercifully drenched in sweat.

The moral of the story is that we can't control everything in life. Sure, we all *know* that, but when it really comes down to a specific hair-raising moment, it is amazing how quickly we absorb that fact.

And, actually, it is quite freeing.

LETTING GO

After we have done everything we can to produce an outcome — put the pieces in place, made sure the cogs in the machinery are working, done our huge self-preparation, tried to forecast any negative outcomes — we simply need to let go. However, that is not usually what we do.

We try to control every little aspect to make sure that our end result conforms exactly to what we had hoped. But what if there is a better result out there than what we had imagined?

If we try to squeeze circumstances and events dry with our control, there is no room for magical things to happen. When this occurs, we do not even produce close to the results that we wished for in the first place.

After our preparations, we must let go.

In our letting go and trusting that 'things will work out', events have a chance to recombine themselves in ways that would be impossible for us to imagine, since we cannot know all the mysterious variables that exist.

Sitting in a hotel in New Hampshire with all their belongings parked in a trailer attached to their car, Marilyn, a fabric designer and her architect husband, Thomas, did not have a definite idea where they were going when they had started driving from their previous home in Utah. They had driven with the idea of starting a new life on the east coast of the United States with no exact idea of how, what, where or anything else about it. It was not their usual modus operandi, but there it was. After knocking about in the afternoon at a local college, and asking everyone they met about rentals, they were just about to give up and leave for the day, when someone ran up to them with a piece of paper on which was written the telephone number of a person interested in renting out their house.

Long story short, it was a fascinating couple who not only rented them their home (while the owners planned to live for six months in a foreign country) but included (along with a list of people like a plumber and electrician to fix anything for the house) an entire list of their friends, with whom Marilyn and Thomas subsequently had the most magical experiences in the year they lived in New Hampshire. It would have been impossible to orchestrate such happenings, but simply by trying their best and then letting it go, the pieces of the tapestry wove themselves.

WHEN THINGS ARE GOING WELL

Letting ourselves trust in the unknown in less-than-optimal circumstances is not the only kind of trust that benefits us. We also need to learn how to trust when things go well!

> *When we do everything we can, and then let the wind carry the seeds, usually something gets planted in a very fortuitous place.*

Sometimes when life gives us exactly what we wish, we then start to worry that it will be taken away. *Sometimes the fear of losing something prevents us from even having it in the first place!*

Therefore, we need to learn to trust in joy as well. To dispel the notion that something negative may happen to us because we have received something wonderful. There is no outside punishment for being happy or for receiving what we have wished. The only judgment comes from ourselves ...

To trust in joy and positive outcomes means that we fully accept physically, mentally, emotionally and spiritually all the good that is coming to us, and can even imagine more of the same, without feeling guilty or self-judgmental.

I'm not saying it is easy to trust in negative or positive situations, but I have found that when we do everything we can, and then let the wind carry the seeds, usually something gets planted in a very fortuitous place.

What does this have to do with creativity? A lot. Creativity is not only that which we make or do. Creativity is the very fiber of our being, and learning how to let creative forces flow is the most wonderful thing we can do for ourselves and others. Trust is a creative force. Trust in ourselves and our capabilities to bring forth that which desires to be born.

28.
Feeling the wish

" "

Destiny grants us our wishes, but in its own way, in order to give us something beyond our wishes.

Johann Wolfgang von Goethe

In many fairy tales the gift of 'three magical wishes' seems to appear as a powerful ingredient. These supernatural declarations usually have great significance for the story in terms of what is desired, who has uttered them, and what the possible consequences may be.

Generally speaking, it often turns out that after huge peaks and valleys of fantastical adventures the want is fulfilled, but in a slightly different and usually better way than the original wish.

With our desires and wishes, it is indeed important to remember that the universe has thousands of possible story lines as to how it can fulfill our dreams and longings. For us to concentrate on only one particular outcome as being the *only* way that our wish may materialize is tremendously limiting when you are dealing with the grand scheme of quantum possibilities!

Therefore we visualize, hope, dream, practice our incantations and affirmations, participate in meditations and create vision boards, all of which are excellent, but only preparatory, for the work that lies ahead. That work consists of doing all the actions we can think of to reach our goals, since the universe works in *partnership.* We cannot sit back and expect a delivery without doing our share of labor.

We also need to understand that when we desire something, we cannot at the same time be thinking, 'Oh, I don't deserve', or 'It's not really possible'. In other words, we cannot desire something and at the same time be negating the possibility that we can have it, for this is the surest way to block the receiving of our desires or the visit of the muse! We would not put birthday cake in front of someone we love and then say they may not eat it! You *can* have your cake and eat it too!

> *In order to manifest a future we have not as yet physically encountered, it is important to understand that we must live that future now.*

It is vitally important that what we desire is something we profoundly and solidly believe we can have. It is not something we wish we could have, but a conviction and belief that it is something we deserve and are prepared to accept 100 per cent!

This sounds very simple!

And it is, except that about 90 per cent of people are not able to believe in themselves or their abilities to receive, either materially or creatively.

In order to manifest a future we have not as yet physically encountered, it is important to understand that we must live that future now, regardless of whether or not it is a part of our present reality.

How do we do that?

START FROM THE END RESULT

When we visualize, this uses only one of the senses we possess. If we visualize a new business, we usually see it only as something in our mind's eye. However, from there we need to fill in the picture with many more details, provided by our other senses.

Perhaps it is a type of enterprise that serves people relocating to foreign destinations for work purposes. We might see ourselves in a beautiful airy office working with clients and allaying their concerns about the mundane matters of a large move. But most important we start to *feel* and live that life in our imagination and our present life.

We begin to recognize that scenario as something which has *already* occurred.

We feel the satisfaction in our bodies when we have helped a family make a successful transition. We hear the reassuring and knowledgeable way we speak to our clients. We feel secure monetarily since our business has a wonderful track record of success. We feel grateful and happy at the beautiful testimonials we receive about the trust and satisfaction felt for our services. We feel fantastic because we are able to look beyond our work to contribute philanthropically to causes outside of the business. We feel at peace, energized and committed to ourselves, our family and our clients. All these feelings are deeply ingrained and living in our bodies.

When that reality becomes as true in our bodies as our present reality, then we have indeed lived the future. At that moment, we are no longer looking through the window from the outside but are actually experiencing all the feelings and emotions of our fulfilled dream.

That is starting from the end result.

Our energy is the catalyst that causes events to begin moving into the forms we wish.

Like molten gold into a cast, our wishes and dreams begin to flow into the shape for which they were intended.

It begins by giving ourselves permission to dream, the confidence to accept and the determination to create what we desire, on an inner and outer level, since that is part of the work which is required to make our dreams a reality.

This is true partnership with the universe, whereby your wishes, perhaps more than three, will be heard, and answered!

29.
Creativity and wellbeing

"

Creativity requires the courage
to let go of certainties.

Erich Fromm

We are born to create.

From the moment we come into this world we start looking around to see what there is, to make sense of our surroundings and to mesh our desires with our environment.

As we grow, we thrive in a constant state of discovery as we begin to use our senses and to create with puzzles, blocks, crayons and paints. We might call it child's play, but it is much more than this simple phrase. It is the sheer joy of moving our realities around to construct new ideas.

Even though I have painted very little in my life, when I enter an art store and see all the myriad types of sable-tipped brushes, oils and acrylic paints, canvases, exotically named tubes of colors, pads of colored papers, my mind starts to salivate as if I was at an all-you-can-eat brunch of visual delicacies. My imagination is seized by my eyes and allowed to run wildly through fabulous possibilities, none of which usually amount to much since my wants are greater than my wallet.

Our urge to create does not stop with kindergarten, however. It continues through life, despite the ferocious, ever ongoing cuts to the 'nonessential' arts programs in schools. Our urge to improve upon that which is and to bring into existence that which is not yet, and to creatively express ourselves through dance, art, music, drama, sports, science, business or the spoken word, our disciplines and every act of our daily life are what keep us moving forward.

If we are not permitted to do this, we become stagnant and sad since even small acts of daily creativity can keep our morale high and give us a sense of control and movement in our lives. In an article in *The Journal of Positive Psychology*, researchers reported on their findings that 'spending time on creative goals during a day is associated with higher activated positive affect (PA) on that day'.[2]

Many people think it is necessary to be a great artist of some sort in order to allow themselves the opportunity to do anything creative. The number of times I have heard, 'Oh I don't have any talent for', 'But what I do is nothing compared to' or 'I can't.' This is just all noise. The kind of noise that the parents' voices in the Charlie Brown TV cartoons used to make. Sort of dull, unintelligible, nonsense that Charles Schultz, the creator of Charlie Brown, so fantastically and wisely used.

Why do people think they have to be 'great, talented, impressive' etc. to allow themselves access to their own creativity?

Judgment. From themselves, and others.

But judgment from ourselves or others is a real killer. Of possibility, learning, joy, discovery and fun! Having spoken about judgment elsewhere in this book, my fervent hope is that it does not become the deciding factor in whether you should, or should not, pursue a large or small creative passion. Nor stop you from the expression of an idea which might in some way change the world!

WHAT IS CREATIVITY?

So, what actually is creativity? And why should we bother about it when there are so many other 'important' things in the world?

> "

Creativity is a combinatorial force: it's our ability to tap into our 'inner' pool of resources — knowledge, insight, information, inspiration and all the fragments populating our minds — that we've accumulated over the years just by being present and alive and awake to the world and to combine them in extraordinary new ways.

Maria Popova, Brain Pickings

Everything we experience in our world is either a creative function of nature or of humankind.

How can we believe that creativity is not fundamental to our lives when we look around and notice the environment in which we live? Taking it a step further, are not our own personal expressions, even a misshapen piece of pottery, not as important as an iPhone? Perhaps not to the world, but to ourselves and our psyche, it is crucial to express the physical and energetic blueprints that were with us when we came.

And it's not only ourselves.

CREATIVITY AS THE KEY TO THE FUTURE

In his book *A Whole New Mind: Why right-brainers will rule the future*, Daniel Pink states that the 'soft' skills of the right brain such as compassion, understanding and empathy will take the place of our typical left-brain linear, bottom-line thinking, thus becoming the driving forces for the creativity, inventiveness and success of future business. Creativity will be the deciding factor in business competition.

In 2010, IBM's 'Global CEO Study' surveyed 1500 CEOS from 60 countries and 33 industries. Based on the answers the CEOs gave, the study concluded that 'more than rigor, management discipline, integrity or even vision — successfully navigating an increasingly complex world will require creativity'.[3] A 2016 report from the World Economic Forum, titled 'The Future of Jobs', came to a similar finding: 'Creativity will become one of the top three skills workers will need. With the avalanche of new products, new technologies and new ways of working, workers are going to have to become more creative in order to benefit from these changes.'⁴ These are sea changes.

> *"*
>
> *The economic future of an organization depends on its ability to create wealth by fostering innovation, creativity and entrepreneurship.*
>
> Linda Naiman

FLEXING YOUR CREATIVE MUSCLE

How to be creative? Can we learn creativity?

Contrary to what we might have been taught, creativity is not doled out to a select few people with the rest of the population dragging along behind as dull and untalented blobs. Being creative takes work, like anything else, but it can be easier for some more than others only because of the former's *habit* of thinking in a certain manner.

In fact, creativity is very much like a muscle. The more you use it, the stronger it gets. It is a way of looking at the world, of bringing disparate pieces of information together to create something different. Taking new ideas and making them a reality, just the way you did when you were two years old.

Some ideas to teach yourself to see and think differently.

Take a situation and look at it from as many angles as possible, in order to reinterpret it in multiple ways. The object is to move away from what might be your regular, or go-to, point of view.

Experiment with different solutions in your mind to a given problem. You are not looking for *the* solution but for varying possibilities.

Schedule some 'playtime' with your imagination concerning a project or goal and be sure not to inhibit or judge your visions no matter how crazy they might seem.

Try some completely different activity no matter how much it 'isn't you' for the purpose of getting out of your regular headspace. I once got a real insight about something important that only occurred to me at a moment when I was participating in rock climbing (which, for me, was really frightening). I'm not saying you need to do something scary; it just happened that at that particular moment, my fear opened up some other part of me and enabled a new insight.

In general, learn new things. Become a beginner again. Not just to *experience* new things, but to actually *learn* something new, which literally creates new neurons in your brain. The larger your base of information, the more building blocks you have for your ideas and imagination.

OTHER BENEFITS OF CREATIVITY

It turns out that there are physical benefits to creativity as well.

A 2014 review, cited in *Medical News Today*, found that people with musical training show a greater connection between the brain's two hemispheres.[5] Another study discovered that older people experienced improvements in both psychological wellbeing and cognitive function — specifically their problem-solving abilities and recall — after four weeks of taking part in theater performances.[6,7]

In terms of what creativity can do for our physical and emotional selves, and for the world at large, it seems this should be the number one course experienced and taught from early age onwards!

And if you think creativity has nothing to do with corporate business success or other fields, let me assure you that it does!

At one time I knew a rather well-known conductor who was used to dealing with large numbers of people in the daily work of his own opera company: orchestral musicians, singers, stagehands, scenic designers, prompters, costume designers, make up artists and others. He had dealt with many mishaps onstage during the years — late entrances of soloists, scenery mishaps, singers who disappeared when they should appear, lighting fiascos and, my particular favorite, when an imported camel lounging backstage stuck its head straight through the scenery of a pyramid, thus facing the audience while making indiscreet camel noises. As the show had to 'carry on', it took an enormous amount of psychological agility to mitigate the disasters of the moment, and to continue with brave and resolute determination to the end. His many stories could have been made into wonderful comedic movies.

At some earlier point in his career, he had been drafted into the army and found to his surprise that the platoon commander singled him out during a particularly difficult situation, since he showed such *exceptional and quick-thinking organizational skills* that far outshone anyone around him!

What we learn in one arena helps us in all aspects of life.

Therefore, to saturate ourselves with as many different experiences as we can is the best way to fuel ourselves for the most individual, exciting and rewarding life paths possible!

30.
The world needs *you*

" "

*Your time is limited, so don't waste it living someone
else's life. Don't be trapped by dogma — which is
living with the results of other people's thinking.
Don't let the noise of others' opinions drown out
your own inner voice. And most important, have
the courage to follow your heart and intuition.*

Steve Jobs

As you have probably figured out by now, creativity is not just
something we do in our spare time. It is the very backbone of our
way of living.

It can be an impulse to create something in the scientific,
business, artistic or other realms, but it really has to do with how

you live life on a daily basis. What thoughts do you live by? What scripts do you follow without even being aware of them, and how can you alter those lines to reflect more truly who you really are?

Our minds are canvases upon which we paint, and our belief systems the palette of colors that we choose.

Since we all have completely different backgrounds and experiences, it is vital to try as best we can to understand ourselves before we can open our gifts to serve others.

Only in plumbing the depths of our own being can we help others to do the same. Not because we wish to bring them to our way of thinking, but rather to understand what may be common to many, while respecting the individuality of all.

> *Our minds are canvases upon which we paint, and our belief systems the palette of colors that we choose.*

It is easy to find yourself in a rut, especially in later years when new experiences are not the norm. Therefore, to find out and expand who you are, it is necessary to come out of your usual routine, even if it seems in the beginning a little artificial to do so.

Let me tell you about two remarkable people who live on several acres of forest on the east coast of the United States. One is a superb actor known for her many professional talents, and the other, a writer of wisdom and eloquence. Both are known for their out-of-this-world cooking (which I have had the pleasure

204

of tasting!), as well as their extraordinarily warm and generous hearts (which I have had the pleasure of experiencing).

A charmed existence has not been their experience, since they have had more than their fair share of life difficulties, but they have managed with grace and determination to keep buoyant upon the waves of life. I do not mention these wonderful spirits because of their innate talent, for that is almost irrelevant, but because of the creative muse that nourishes them and everyone else in their circle.

On their acres of woodland, they produced an annual 'spectacle' that involved quite a number of people. A trail was laid through the thick forest, with each twist and turn culminating in a verdant, fragrant grove of trees large or small, equipped with wooden platforms and small colored lights twinkling enticingly in the evening breeze.

At each destination one found a performance of music, dance or perhaps a tableau, based upon the general theme for that year, all nestled against a background of summer dusk and fireflies. The costumed actors, who were all neighbors, friends or townspeople, created the props and scenery, which allowed each person to display their own creative morsels, contributing to the richness of the whole.

This 'spectacle' was created every season for more than 20 years, with the couple spending most of the preceding year creating the masterpiece in time for its summer inception. They understood that to be supported by the muse, one must be ready to undertake the work required, for it will only join us when it feels we have come at least halfway!

The most wonderful thing about the entire event was how it

released inner treasure from every single person who participated (which meant the entire village) and wove these jewels into a marvelous experiential tapestry for the forest walkers.

In other words, by dancing with their muse our friends were able to not only nourish themselves, but to bring healing and uplifting to an entire population.

If this sounds magical, indeed it was, for I have not encountered anything like it since. It taught me how much we can inspire others when we inspire ourselves first.

However, you don't need to be 'talented' to change the world. None of those townspeople were hugely talented in the conventional sense. But what was so uplifting was the sincerity and nobleness that came from each one of them as they poured out their personalities and energies into the soup of creativity. And that was what made it so amazing, touching and utterly compelling.

Each of us has something to say, expressed in whatever form is natural to our being. In drinking from our own wellspring of creativity we discover new possibilities within us, producing fresh thoughts and actions.

Nothing can be more intrinsically interesting than finding out something new about ourselves. It can be amusing, exciting or disheartening, but the mere discovery means that we have more information to work with in terms of enlarging our beings.

> *Each of us has something to say, expressed in whatever form is natural to our being.*

It is my sincere hope that this book has helped you realize how you can learn to trust your creative visions. Not just for the external events of life, but for your inner ability to ride the winds of chaos and uncertainty that batter all of us from time to time.

By getting to know our inner selves through acts of creativity either involving ourselves or others, we peer into the storehouse of our own treasures and gifts, thus preventing us from succumbing to emotional maelstroms and the incapacitating furies of, among others, sorrow, despair, fear and hate.

In the development of our capabilities we come upon new solutions, new ways of thinking that perhaps would have been less available had we not consistently pushed ourselves down new, and perhaps uncomfortable, paths.

Stagnation of thought and resistance to new ideas has always been one of humankind's weaknesses, leading to frustration and mind paralysis. Creativity during overwhelming times, pandemics, loss, grief is crucial to our human spirit if we are to continue to have a world that has a chance of expressing its highest potential. It is only creativity that will solve such problems as hunger, sorrow, illness and war.

Being curious and moving towards our future selves is the first step towards opening the potentials with which we arrived. To harvest our gifts means we must move beyond our fears into mental scenarios which may seem at first like strange places, until we acclimatize ourselves to the fact that they are real possibilities that always existed. However, we can only see things we are ready to see, and in order to make that happen we must start with our inner vision.

> *Being curious and moving towards our future selves is the first step towards opening the potentials with which we arrived.*

Beginning with ourselves in small ways, with curiosity and kindness and encouraging others to do the same is the start of a new way of being that will ripple far beyond our creative pursuits. In the expression of the human soul lies the key to self-esteem, kindness and the urge to help others in whatever way they need.

Therefore, creativity becomes fundamentally how you use your life force.

Creativity starts in the mind, for what you think determines what happens in the next instant as well as the rest of your life. How we marshal the powers of our mind to serve our desires and goals is what determines our personal success. Mind defines destiny.

The reply to 'Why are we here?' lies in the path of creativity and imagination. In your desires live your answers. In your visions reside your future.

The emotional freedom that will come from releasing fear as you discover new horizons of possibilities, along with the heartfelt embrace of what is intrinsically yours, will not only transform yourself but your life.

To that end, I wish you a beautiful journey!

Acknowledgments

Great appreciation and thanks to Gareth St John Thomas, founder and CEO of Exisle Publishing for providing my first ever phone call from New Zealand (!) and for delivering the wonderful news that he would be taking *Dancing with Your Muse* under his wing.

My sincere thanks to Anouska Jones, publishing and editorial director at Exisle Publishing for her never-ending graciousness and patience in answering all my questions, several times a day, thus making me feel as if I was the only person that mattered in the entire publishing house!

To my editor, Karen Gee, who has the uncanny ability to feel and speak in the author's voice, resulting in seamless suggestions and smoothed terrain. I am exceedingly grateful.

Thank you to everyone at Exisle Publishing who has helped bring my book into the world, with a special mention of Enni Tuomisalo for her exuberant cover design so aptly depicting the creative spirit.

A special thank you to Michael J. Chase, best-selling author and renowned speaker as well as treasured friend and mentor, whose unceasing support and encouragement made this book a reality.

My heartfelt thanks to former students and clients who have honored me with their openness and trust and allowed me to share their stories.

And finally, my greatest appreciation and thanks to my husband Nik, for his endless patient re-reads in a non-native language, enduring good humor, constant support and grace.

Endnotes

1. Guren, J. 'Nureyev: 'I am an intruder', *New York Times*, 5 May 1974.

2. Tamlin, S., Conner, T.S., Colin, G., DeYoung, C.G., and Silvia, P.J. 2016, 'Everyday creative activity as a path to flourishing', *Journal of Positive Psychology*, vol. 13, issue 2, pp. 181–9.

3. IBM 2010 Global CEO Study: 'Creativity selected as most crucial factor for future success', https://www.creativityatwork.com/2010/05/19/ceo-creativity-leadership-ibm-global-report/

4. World Economic Forum Report: 'The future of jobs report 2016', https://www.weforum.org/reports/the-future-of-jobs-report-2016

5. Moore, E., Schaefer, R.S., Bastin, M.E., Roberts, N., and Over, K. 2014, 'Can musical training influence brain connectivity? Evidence from diffusion tensor MRI', *Brain Sciences*, vol. 4, issue 2, pp. 405–27.

6. Cohut, M. 'What are the health benefits of being creative?', *Medical News Today*, 16 February 2018, https://www.medicalnewstoday.com/articles/320947

7. Noice, H., Noice, T., and Staines, G. 2004, 'A short-term intervention to enhance cognitive and affective functioning in older adults', *Journal of Aging and Health*, https://doi.org/10.1177/0898264304265819

Index